When Kingdoms Fall

A Novel About the Fall of Lucifer

By

Elaine Rose Penn

ISBN: 978-0-9700449-2-1

Back cover photo by Yakeima Yarbrough

Other books by Elaine Rose Penn
Soul Ties
A Chance At Life: Stories of Inspiration and
Hope for Adoptive and Foster Parents
My Soul Looks Back and Wonders: The Call of God
on a Woman's Life
Grave Clothes: A Novel About the Death of Lazarus

The Secret things belong unto the Lord our God: but those things which are revealed belong unto us and to our children forever....
Deuteronomy 29:29a (KJV)

CONTENTS

SECTION ONE: BEFORE IT WAS

SECTION TWO: THE SCEPTER FROM JUDAH

SECTION THREE: IT IS FINISHED

Prologue

The dark, fallen angel rolled over onto his side with searing pain coming from everywhere. He was familiar with sadness, with exasperation, with excitement, with exhilaration, even loss—but there was the addition of a rawness to his psyche and mind that was new and troubling. He kept rolling from side to side trying to figure out something, but then he discovered the strange connection between movement and pain. The rolling seemed to increase the agonizing ache, and he discovered the strange sensation of not being able to connect. He couldn't touch but he could feel, and that began to bother him more than the pain inside.

There was a disconnect of some kind—between his self and his inner self...he kept shifting himself gently by inches to gain his bearing or at least to come to a sitting position...but he couldn't. Finally, he lay still trying to remember...trying to grasp a hold of happenings, and incidents, and sights and sounds. Oh! With a jolt, he remembered something...a terrible conflict, was it? As he tried to grab the memory so that he could look at it and examine it, he found himself in a kneeling position with pain stabbing and jabbing him with relentless accuracy. To counter the assault, he tried to wrap himself up in his own arms, but could not connect, and went back to a prone, rolling position. Now, he quickly became afraid. Why was he unable to touch his own body? He had limbs, but yet he didn't!

Something in the shadows seemed to move. Or had he imagined it? He was surprised to see a pair of eyes staring at him. Oddly, they touched a nerve with him and activated a mixture of fear, awe, and disdain. He peered up at the eyes and had to fight the sensation that he had been surrounded and overcome. The eyes were just standing there watching him. Were these eyes responsible for his pain?

They were a strange pair of eyes...more than just orbs of light, they were prodding eyes...inquiring eyes...but mostly they seemed to hold him captive. They seemed to be the eyes of a lone figure standing still in the darkness, watching him, even chiding him. As he shifted weightless body mass trying to ease the pressure of all-consuming pain, the eyes began to bother him. He turned toward the eyes once again and this time he tried to speak to the eyes, but only a small cry came out. Just then, the strange, magnetic eyes took a step backward and were suddenly gone…the inquiry was over. Enough information had been gathered for a report.

The lone beaten figure was actually not alone. An innumerable company of angelic warriors surrounded him. Their presence was cloaked from the dark, wounded figure. However, they were actually—in distance—several hundred miles away from him. They too had been standing there watching to assess as well as to study. He had once been their prince—they looked upon him with a restrained reverence—he was now the vanquished, as well as the spectacle.

His whole appearance had changed and as he lay before them, it kept shifting and rolling in a perverse display of degradation and darkness. It seemed as if he were metamorphosing into something frightening and unnatural. The questions swirled in their minds – what was he experiencing and where was his once magnificent body? His roiling and cries of stifled agony were sometimes broken by a sudden stillness in his movements. He startled them when momentarily he jolted into a kneeling position, but then just as quickly he crumpled into a mass of deformed body mass as his metamorphosing robbed him of any control.

His fall had been an indignant one and had caused catastrophic damage to the atmospheric and stellar heavens. The damage to the earth was astounding. What a sight it had been. They kept their eyes trained on the vanquished cherubim as well as the Son of God. They were waiting to know what to do next and anxious to move the fight to the next level. All of them stared in amazement when the vanquished leader made eye contact with the Son. They knew he couldn't see them, but they were nonetheless surprised to see that he could see the

Son. Their eyes seemed locked. What did each think about the other? Did the vanquished now reverence the Lord? Momentarily, they watched the Son as he watched the vanquished. All of a sudden, the Son turned and moved toward them, giving them the signal to retreat. Nothing would ever be the same and the feeling of impending doom to the earth was matched by the very catastrophic damage that had occurred as a result of Lucifer's fall.

Section One

Before It Was

Chapter 1: The Conspiracy

When the heavens split open at the fury of the fall, the earth screamed with a violent casting off. The order of the universe was changed in a moment, and where there had once been calm and beauty, there was now bleak darkness, the water covered the deep, and the first and second heavens hung in shreds upon their axis. The sound, however, was the worse. From nowhere, yet from everywhere, a deafening noise of beating kept cadence with a rhythm of its own. The co-mingling of hue-less colors, intense heat and vapors, and the shrill cadence of a dying earth-heart, made the surrounding worlds unrecognizable. It was hard to imagine that all of this started with an incredibly bold lie.

On the day that the conspiracy first came to the light of day, line upon line of the heavenly hosts had been commanded to appear in formation. Dunastes, an arch commander over ten thousand times ten thousands and thousands of thousands of the heavenly hosts marched at the head of the expansive legions. He struggled to maintain his composure. His name was known in Earth as "Valiant" and it was an accurate description of his military prowess.

He was an imposing figure at thirteen feet in stature, with eyes that pierced like a lance, and a voice that rumbled like thunder. He moved with speeds that far exceeded his equals, and when extended in flight, his wings—from tip to tip—could reach an expanse of twenty-four feet in length. His ornately decorated mantle was the color of crimson, denoting an officer of considerable rank. The emerald, carbuncle, and chrysoprasus garnished the crest of his breastplate; the color of his shin greaves was gold emboldened with purple. His choice of weaponry was the gladius, a two feet long, double-bladed sword, which was the favorite of horsemen for the advantage it gave in mounted combat. Fixed to his girdle was the pugio, a long dagger that he notched with each victory that he won. He never left his abode without it.

As the powerfully built commander surveyed the staging arena, it was the fact that the standards were misarranged in the columns that first caught his attention. The eagle standards were where the unicorns ought to have been, the peacocks were where the lions were always positioned, and the leviathan was missing altogether. If this were not enough, there was an air of intrigue that needled the old officer. Something was afoot, but he was not the one to be toyed with. He signaled for Yibsam, his second in command, to move the front lines forward. The quick hand movement seemed to catch Yibsam off guard. Annoyed, Dunastes repeated the signal. Yibsam spun on his horse and rode toward the arch commander, deliberately ignoring the signal.

"Sir, we are all here and ready to do your bidding. May I inquire as to the reason for the delay in our plans?"

Dunastes bristled at the blatant disregard of his order, but the query bothered him more. *Our plans? Of what did Yibsam refer?* He had been sent a command directly from Prince Lucifer to have the elite brigades of the cavalry militia report in formation and nothing more. He chose not to betray his ignorance of Yibsam's puzzling words.

"Just do as I have asked," was the flat response.

Line upon line, the angelic horsemen, mounted on non-descript stallions, began to march forward under the fixed gaze of the valiant top commander. He studied each with great interest, wondering if they too felt the strange new energy in the air. Each warrior, bright with glory, sat mounted in full battle regalia, the magnificent insignia of their crests and standards signifying their great rank and stature. They were dressed in fine, pure white linen with collars that ran down the center of their breastbone. Their garments were fastened at the waist with a girdle then fell straight down loosely past the shin. Each was outfitted with their favored weapon of choice, sheathed in bronze scabbards at their sides. Their wings were short in breadth and comprised of finely textured hair rather than feathers, and the sound of their marching in time could be terrible as of many chariots running in battle.

Their features were finely chiseled like porcelain and bore no emotion, and some dared with a direct gaze—to look Dunastes right in his eyes. This was new—they had never done that before. The commander caught the daring gesture of many of them and it bothered him greatly. There was something insinuated, yet not outright enough to show disrespect. These were the most valiant of the hosts; each was a commander in his own right. As Yibsam kept signaling line after line to move forward, with a slight nod of his head, Dunastes ordered the parade to cease. He'd had enough. He didn't know how to feel, and it bothered him to no end that the change in the atmosphere seemed imperceptible to everyone else but him. Or so, he thought.

Again, Yibsam moved quickly to the commander. This time his face was drawn with anxiety. Yibsam wondered if Dunastes knew what *he* knew. Surely, Lucifer would have included him. Why was the commander stalling the next step? It was critical that everything go according to plan. There was no room for error. Although the plan had been hatched rather quickly, some of the most stalwart of Michael's fighting captains had thrown in their lot with Lucifer. Some bore the rank of principalities, and still others were rulers over rulers. Each would be needed because of his respective sphere of influence.

This Dunastes, although ranked among the eldest of the captains and high up in Michael's chain of command, was fierce in his loyalty to Lucifer. It seemed unlikely that Lucifer would not have included him. Yibsam wondered momentarily if perhaps it was all a ruse— maybe a part of the plan. Still, he had been cautioned to proceed carefully in the face of any show of resistance. He would let Dunastes be the first to show his hand.

Dunastes had always been considered by most as somewhat of an eccentric. Had he been a human, he would have been described as crusty and hard-bitten. He had reputation among the commanders as a gunslinger of sorts, and seemed to get great pleasure in inflicting pain just to prove a point. His reputation for prowess and strength was undisputed and he made sport of anyone who dared take him on. Some did, hoping to humble him. Of those who held rank as arch commanders, Dunastes was second to none. He was robust even by heaven's standard, and had a mind like a trap door. If you missed, he wouldn't and there was no second strike against him. As a chief commander, he was not one who would likely show his hand unless his foot was securely on your neck.

As he approached the elder commander, Yibsam carefully weighed his options. A misstep could be very costly at this stage of the plot. At Yibsam's approach, Dunastes turned to scrutinize the strange odor that seemed to cling to the worship warrior, whose name meant "Fragrance."

"Sir," Yibsam began in deference, "what are your orders? We stand waiting to do your bidding."

The venerable commander caught the strange mix of caution and overconfidence in the underling's manner. He thought it stranger still, that Yibsam would try to hide it. Was that something akin to contempt that he saw in Yibsam? The emotion was so novel that it was quickly cast aside as a misjudgment. Dunastes used his peripheral vision to weigh Yibsam's demeanor against that of the others and noticed a division in the outlying ranks. There was nervous movement in the inner core of the columns, but not as much as on the peripheries. He had noticed it before as they marched in formation, but now it seemed to have its own face. Soon, it would have its own name. Something was about to go down that would change heaven and earth forever. Dunastes discerned it, but would never comprehend the full details of its origin. His quick-wittedness would have drastic consequences for the conspirators and turn the whole plot upside down.

"Yibsam, do something for me," he started. "Give the command for the columns to divide in armies of two. Have the rear corps face the forward corps as in a direct frontal assault. Stretch them out in battle line array. Do what I say quickly."

When Dunastes noticed the instant consternation of the underling, instinctively he knew that he had hit a nerve. With a good dose of acid, Dunastes gave Yibsam a piercing look and spat out, "Now, not later!"

As the great commander climbed to mount his horse, he whirled around for show with the animal's nostrils flaring. He noticed a greater increase in movement in the distant ranks as if they too could sense his plan to thwart their plan. The nervous energy was so palpable you had to be asleep not to notice it. This had better be a war game, Dunastes thought to himself, or somebody is going to get hurt today! For sure, whatever was about to go down was no longer advantaged by the element of surprise.

Although he relished the thought of a contest with one of the other arch commanders, he couldn't shake the brooding weight of something that was new and entirely foreign. It had a smell to it. The old captain was highly intelligent and discerning. He didn't know what he was dealing with, but he knew that it was big. As he turned to move away, he made sure Yibsam caught the sound of metal against metal as he yanked his sword from its bronze scabbard. He held it high for all to see and deliberately brandished it upward in the frontal call-for-attack position.

The gesture got the intended effect and Dunastes took note of the fact that it elicited more nervous movement on the edges of the columns than in the middle. Still, the inner cores held stable. Whatever was about to go down, he surmised, would be activated from the outer lines. He made a mental note of the warriors who held those positions and was momentarily intrigued that they were there at all. Usually, these particular captains preferred the front lines rather than the outer perimeters.

Yibsam was flabbergasted. He didn't know which to react to first: the trick Dunastes had just pulled with his sword, or the command he had just given. He knew that by dividing the columns, he would split those that were compatriots in unequal bands. They had taken pains to position friend and foe in the formation lines, such that they would have the advantage of surprise and economy of strength. A parallel formation would equalize the balance and undermine the ambush maneuver, known in tactical combat as a salient.

Yibsam understood the gravity of his responsibility to make sure nothing went wrong. The thing that was now obvious to him, but also bewildering, was the fact that Dunastes was clearly not a part of the plot. The idea that the old commander might not be a part of the allegiance took Yibsam's breath away. This meant that he, Yibsam, would have to neutralize Dunastes. He was no match for the commander in brute strength, but he felt that he could match him in wits. Yibsam was greatly mistaken in this. Dunastes could outfox him with both hands behind his back and standing on one foot.

Yibsam's transformation had already begun. Like Lucifer, he seemed completely unaware that God had not only disenfranchised him, but also repossessed his name. As he became more and more embroiled in the plot to make Lucifer the sovereign of all, he of course was the first to notice the strange odor that emanated from his body. He was greatly discomfited to realize that with the odor came a hardening of his outer skin. It was beginning to turn scaly, and looked like something he had never seen before. At first, the foul smell bothered him because it was new, but then he got used to it. He took comfort in the fact that no else seemed to notice it. Actually, the ones who got close enough to notice did, but they were too engrossed in the repulsiveness of their own changing to care.

Although he was no match for Dunastes, he was no bantamweight either. Yibsam, too, was held in repute among the chief commanders. He was daring, brutish in his power, and quick-tempered. His Achilles heel was that he hated contests and tended to overcompensate by over thinking his next move. Had he learned to trust his own experience in battle, he would have won more than he tended to lose. Still, he was a formidable senior officer, and served Lucifer faithfully as one of his inner circle. He was also fearless, and for this reason was especially selected to move this part of the plan into action first.

By positioning the strongest rulers on the edges, once the signal was given, these would lead their brigades outward and around to achieve a flanking maneuver of the main hosts on three sides. The opponents who were positioned at the front and open side of the salient would join the foray without clear direction of where the attack was coming from, actually making things worse, by instinctively moving inward against their own brothers.

The move was intended to catch their opponents off guard and give those positioned in the middle of each column the wherewithal to drive their opponents inward to attack each other in confusion. They would not know from which direction the assault was concentrated, because foe would look and act like friend, each singularly taking advantage of the confusion. Then they would strike with decisive force, crippling their opponent, taking them captive, and thereby stripping them of the advantage they held in their superior numbers. The plan would have worked except for one oversight, namely, Dunastes.

Just when Yibsam could delay response to the command no longer, they were both struck with awe when they caught sight of Lucifer walking back and forth as if inspecting, from the rear of the massive columns. You would never miss him because of the glory that enveloped him–his very being was brighter than the Northern Lights. It was Dunastes who actually saw him first, and was shocked by what he saw.

Lucifer moved with lightning speed from the rear guard of the columns to the foremost. He was on foot, and this alone was mind-boggling as Lucifer never walked–he was always either exalted on his throne of which the Earth was his dominion, or he was prostrate in worship at the foot of God's throne. From henceforth, he would be cursed to walk incessantly. He would always be on the move.

Dunastes stared at him as he approached, and was thankful that he had sufficient time to study the changes in his prince. Normally, Lucifer's beauty could take your breath away, no matter how many times you saw him. His breast consisted of tabrets and musical pipes, encrusted with weighty fine jewels. In stunning contrast, a vesture draped his massive body overlaid with colorful precious stones of the heavenly rainbow in sardius, topaz, diamond and beryl, the onyx – eye of the great tiger, jasper, sapphire and emerald, carbuncle and gold.

An ancient and mysterious color of heaven called *melek* which signified royalty, adorned the fringes of each layer of his vestment. Draped about his fingers were heralding instruments of the psaltery and kinnor, fastened with golden cords. Pressed oil made of Cassia and Bdellium anointed his rich, embroidered locks and skin. The tabrets, which comprised his vocal chords, could ascend into cadences of the dulcimer and harp, and then drop suddenly to the lower reaches of the shophar. He was full of wisdom and perfect in beauty.

This magnificent[1] angel had one head, but four faces. One face was that of a lion, another was that of an eagle, a third was that of an ox, and the fourth was that of a man. Six sets of wings stretched high above his massive, but elegant head. With two wings, he covered his faces, and with two wings he covered his feet. With the third set of wings, he comported himself about. He was known as Son of the Morning, among the highest rank of cherubim angels and was the first one created by God. This order of angels along with the seraphim had fierce strength, and great splendor and beauty. With their thunderous voices they shook the foundations of the heavens with their cries, "Holy, holy is the Lord of hosts, the whole earth and the heights of the heavens is full of his glory!" He, along with Michael and Gabriel,

---

[1] Ezekiel 1:7-13; 10:14; 28:13-17
Isaiah 6:1-3; 14:12

held the inaugural and military rank of Archangel over the heavenly hosts.

Lucifer's pomp and dignity belied his private affliction. Few knew it, but the reason he walked rather than rode today was the aching pain he felt from head to toe. If he sat it hurt, if he rode it hurt, if he stood, it hurt. Only walking eased the agony. The pain caused great inner turmoil and he could feel an inner shifting of muscles and sinew. The iniquity spreading inside of him had become an onerous cancer.

In spite of the mysterious metamorphosing, he still bore all of his princely regalia. Flanked to the right and left were several of his buccellarii, a contingent of his security detail. To his right were Samach, Tohar, Charash, and Ashedah. To his left and bringing up the rear, Yerach and Yasha. Except for Charash who bore the missing standard of the leviathan, each held a sword in his fighting hand. Dunastes, the angelic champion, took notice of each detail. Something didn't feel right, so Dunastes instinctively clutched his as well. He had never re-sheathed it in its scabbard. Out of respect for his prince Lucifer, however, he held the short thrusting blade in his left hand in the rest position upward and crisscrossing his breastbone.

Without hesitating, both Dunastes and Yibsam dismounted their horses, went down each to his left knee, striking their balled fist against their hearts. They lowered their head then lifted it in unison, as was their customary salute to cherubim and seraphim. Lucifer signaled acknowledgement of the salute and nodded for them to stand. Dunastes was stunned by the quivering twitch in Lucifer's faces. He had to control his jaw from dropping. Something akin to horror swept over Dunastes. What was he seeing? What was happening this day? What did this all mean?

As he stared at what had always been a very powerful visage, he was stunned to see that Lucifer's brightness was no longer bright. The thought came to Dunastes that the one who stood before him was no longer the Son of the Morning.

"All hail, Malak Yahweh, Prince Lucifer. Is it well with you?" the old captain ventured as he gripped Lucifer's shoulder as a sign of affection.

"Dunastes, Chief Commander of the Sabaoth, it is well with me, and assuredly with you," came the slow reply—Dunastes' grip had sent shards of pain from the neck to the sternum.

Lucifer seemed to have to steady himself and his vocal chords sounded altered. But before he could say more, a sudden movement from behind startled all of them. This would be a day full of surprises.

It was Otsmah who had broken ranks to flank Dunastes on his right. Behind him came Sebazomai and Shachah. All three were mounted with swords drawn. The gesture was disrespectful to say the least. Lucifer roared with rage and when he did, a strange dark cloak wound tightly about his vestment sagged, exposing a large gaping wound in his throat. There was massive discoloration around his neck and the lower jaw of all of his faces. Although the tabrets and pipes on first glance looked intact, many of the stones in his priestly tunic, the Urim and Thummim, were missing. For a moment, time stood still and Dunastes knew there and in that moment that the magnificent Archangel Lucifer, the one that he honored and even adored, had been defrocked. His mind reeled with the enormity of it.

The weight of the realization was nearly too much. With the shock came a feeling of dread as well as sorrow. He was glad for the interruption, no matter the extent of the insult. He needed a moment to think. He couldn't fight the feeling that something was about to go down. He was determined to be neither pawn nor prey. Whichever way this thing was about to go down, one thing was certain, he was and would always be a captain of Elohim, the Chief Commander of Sabaoth. If he had to hurt somebody to provide evidence, it wouldn't be the first time. He switched the sword from his left hand to his fighting hand, clutched the hilt of his blade tighter, and deliberately stepped back to balance his body weight. Throughout the immeasurable columns, those who knew Dunastes well took note of the move, and with the cunning instinct of warriors, prepared for a brawl. Lucifer saw it too.

"Dunastes, order your lieutenants to stand down!" bellowed Lucifer.

Yibsam, who still stood beside the elder captain, was too overcome with shock at the boldness of the move to speak. Finally, he found his voice. "Otsmah, Sebazomai, Shachah, what do you mean by this insult against the Lord's Prince? For this, you shall pay dearly, all three of you!"

In a calm, measured voice, Dunastes turned to the three young rulers and gave a terse command for them to dismount, "Do it."

Otsmah spoke first, never showing any deference for Lucifer, and by degrees even less toward the arch commander. "Dunastes, we have an urgent message from Prince Michael. He sends orders for you to come to him without delay."

Dunastes had been mistaken. As he peered at them, he realized that they had been absent from the formation all along. How was it that he had not missed them? Yibsam, although still wired with rage, was thinking the same thought. He too had not missed them. Yibsam had the sinking feeling that things were beginning to unravel. He looked to Lucifer and was disappointed to see that he too had been caught off guard.

"You have one second to order your underlings down, Dunastes," came the measured threat from Lucifer. "I have come this very moment to communicate the matter of which Prince Michael[2] is concerned. Your underlings have overstepped their bounds. Order them to stand down at once!"

---

[2] Daniel 10:13

Again, Dunastes turned to the three who were curiously unmoved by the threat of the great cherubim, Lucifer. They should have been trembling at his feet.

Unknown to Dunastes, Michael had given them strict warning to treat Lucifer as a belligerent. They were instructed to not obey any order given by him, nor were they to give him the salute due a captain of the Lord's hosts. In addition, they were ordered to make no eye contact with him nor were they to address him directly. It was a subtle element that Dunastes did not notice, but Lucifer did. He was there when many of them had been created and he knew that the secret of their great strength as angelic generals was in their strict obedience to commands. The fact that they would so openly defy him was considered high treason. Clearly, they acted in compliance to someone else of an equal or higher rank than he.

Their obstinacy intrigued Dunastes, for they had not submitted to his command either. These were three of his most trusted deputies. Such a gesture of insubordination was unknown in the hosts. It made sense that Prince Michael had sent them as his emissaries. More than once, Dunastes had singled them out for a duel in war games to toughen their resolve. Each took their thrashing without a whimper. They had hearts of steel.

Dunastes turned to face them with a mixture of conflicting emotions. Once these three left the staging arena, he would be here alone with Lucifer and surrounded by opponents. He could not fathom how extensive the conspiracy might be, and without the benefit of reconnaissance did not know who was on the Lord's side. Clearly, Prince Michael knew something, but at the moment he, Dunastes, was in a rather awkward position.

"You will return to Prince Michael and inform him that you have given the command as so ordered. Go without delay. Your assignment here is complete," spoke the commander to the three emissaries.

A plan was taking shape in Dunastes' mind, but he needed more time and more information. The three warriors turned without giving a salute even to Dunastes and rode away swiftly. Both friend and foe had witnessed their act of defiance. The entire arena was stiff with incredulity. Yibsam, who had gone entirely to the other side, was bewildered by the extent of their disregard for Lucifer.

"Dunastes, you dare insult your Prince before the hosts?" queried Lucifer angrily. "Am I not equal to Michael in both rank and power? I gave strict orders for Yibsam to begin war games today and without delay. Why are the cohorts not dissembled for tactics? Jehoshua Yahweh has ordered a highly classified scrutiny of the cavalry. Prince Michael has been tied up with other matters and Jehoshua asked that I communicate the change to you on His behalf. He felt certain of your full cooperation, but instead you have become an obstruction!" He was bluffing but only Yibsam knew the full truth.

This caught Dunastes off guard and he wondered for a moment why Yibsam had not simply said that. Had he not just commanded Yibsam to dissemble for tactics? Lucifer could see the old general mentally weighing the new information against his instinct. This time Lucifer chose his words carefully, and you could tell that he was fighting to match wits with the shrewd commander who stood before him. He felt certain that Dunastes could be handled and the plot moved forward as planned. It was an error in judgment that Dunastes would take full advantage of.

"My Lord, Beelzebul[3], give me leave to deal with Otsmah, Shachah and Sebazomai for their rebellion," pleaded Yibsam who was still boiling with fury.

As if he had room for further shock, Dunastes stood with his mind reeling at the use of the strange title. *What was it that Yibsam had called the Prince? Beelzebul?* The meaning was unclear, but it jolted

---

[3] Matthew 12:24-26

15

back to memory a recent incident that had nagged him greatly when it occurred.

He fought to maintain a straight face and to pretend that he had not heard it. If he were going to match wits with the great cherubim this day, he must be careful to respond and not react to anything said or done. And if all else failed, there was always his blade. He flexed his hand on the handle of his sword again, completely unaware that those who were on the Lord's side throughout the arena were watching his every move and just waiting for him to start something. The conflict had been brewing long before they had been called to formation and the warriors of the Lord were hungry for a fight.

Lucifer was no fool. He knew that Dunastes had heard Yibsam's slip and now realized that his loyal friend and chief commander would have to be neutralized very quickly. He was hoping that it was not too late to recoup what would surely be a great loss to his cause.

"Yibsam," Lucifer spoke in low tones, "you are a fool. Leave Dunastes and I alone for a moment. All of you go. I will call for you in a moment. Continue the inspection of my armies, but start in the rear," spat Lucifer in contempt.

Deflated, Yibsam quickly realized that Dunastes had not only heard the slip, but would perhaps also grasp its implications. He had been the first, after all, to show his hand. It pained him to think that he had failed his god, Beelzebul, lord of dung.

Lucifer, on his part, was dismayed that things were going completely awry. He knew Dunastes well enough to know that he was standing here playing a game of wits. The old captain relished such contests, and it was not beneath him to contrive one for the enjoyment of it all. Lucifer was wearied from the intrigue, as well as the changing, but knew that once his plan had taken shape, that even all of this would make it worth it.

"Dunastes, you have dishonored your prince before the hosts, but I am willing to allow you to make amends to me before them all. If you are for me, fall down now and pay me homage!" cried Lucifer.

Dunastes, momentarily bewildered, stared at Lucifer wondering if the bizarre physical changes affecting the cherubim had affected his mind as well. In point of fact, the changing was indeed affecting his mind.

"My prince," Dunastes began slyly, "although I am most contrite and feel a great responsibility for the actions of my three lieutenants, it is they who should pay you homage for their feigned impudence and not I. Yibsam, though a fool as you have said, is right. They should be dealt with according to their folly. It will also allow me to get to the bottom of their remarkable insolence. I spoke to Prince Michael earlier this morning, and he, too, gave strict orders regarding the secrecy of the war games today. He informed me of the switch in command, but his dispatch of my lieutenants was a part of an elaborate scheme to test their mettle. What they lack in refinement, they have made up for in their acting ability. Your visit here today, though pointless, my lord, has taken all of us by surprise."

Lucifer gazed at Dunastes with renewed interest and secretly admired him. His charm was as smooth as butter. In a different time and place, this Dunastes would have been a great hustler. He realized now what a monumental mistake it had been not to work more diligently to recruit him to his cause.

The con, of course, did not fool Lucifer at all. He felt certain that Yibsam would have informed Dunastes that the call to formation came from him, not Prince Michael and that nothing more regarding the conspiracy had been laid bare. His plans had not been foiled, although Dunastes' filibustering would make it seem so. Moreover, he was sure of what he'd seen in Dunastes' face when the three lieutenants first appeared. He, too, had been taken aback by the summons from Michael, as well as the insolence of his three lieutenants.

Lucifer moved slowly to Dunastes' left as if to encircle him. Dunastes countered by moving with him like the spokes on a wheel. As the two faced off, the atmosphere between them was no longer conciliatory. The old commander knew what an ambush smelled like. Suddenly, things were coming into clearer focus. That Lucifer would commit high treason made no sense to Dunastes, but it did make sense tactically that he would use the guise of war games to do a preemptive strike. That, of course, thought Dunastes, would have to be done over his dead body. He had not earned his rank as chief arch commander of Sabaoth floating on clouds.

Chapter 2: Ambush

Lucifer was in the heaven of heavens in a garden called Eden[4] when he first looked at himself. As was his custom, he enjoyed walking in the Garden of God among lilies, the fertile anise, and the yellow rue and blooming bdellium. The colors of God's floral palette met in a mosaic profusion of reds, blues, yellows, and greens, among sprays of the anemone and the pink blossoms of spikenard and myrrh. His delight were the brilliant hues of emerald, and purple among the saffron, and the clusters of pomegranate which produced lush bursts of orange and gold. Rich green balsam trees lined twin colonnades along the walls of Eden, with the calamus and the kopher serving as underbrush.

The sounds of Eden were just as marvelous, with humming bees waltzing to the sway of blossoms and crickets trumpeting their staccatos to the rhythm of the forests. The sound of running streams of pure blue water served as a gentle backdrop for the cacophonic sounds of the entire orchestra. In the midst of each winding footpath lined with pearls, jacinth, and beryl were fully matured bulbs of red, white, yellow, and pink roses.

In the very center of this incredibly lavish garden stood his favorite tree, a Lebonah, which produced aromatic frankincense for offerings. He would crush its leaves to fill the bowls around the altars and to make oil for anointing his head. Although he was free to eat of its fruit at his will, it was shrouded in mystery and was compassed about with stones of fire. It was heaven's Tree of Eternal Life. Further to the east and veiled also in mystery was a second tree, a Terebinth, called the Tree of the Knowledge of Good and Evil.

One day, while collecting thatches of hyssop, which he used for ceremonial cleansing and to dress his great locks of hair, Lucifer

---

[4] Ezekiel 28:13-14

strode past it with his customary indifference. It was heavy with fruit and a delight to look upon. Not once had it ever captured his fancy or his curiosity, but on this day, it did. As he stared, it entranced him, and the sight of it startled him out of his reverie of worship. He began to ponder the fact that few had access to the Mountain of God, and even fewer had permission to eat the fruit of its trees. Though he was the cherub that covered, inexplicably, God had not entrusted him with the indulgence of this one tree. It was a dangerous train of thought, and by degrees, a fabrication. Nonetheless, the heresy was stimulating, and Lucifer felt strangely liberated by the freedom he permitted himself in entertaining it.

He reached wide with the intent of just touching it to admire it, but it seemed to retract on the vine. Irritated, he grabbed for another, and this one dropped easily into the palm of his hand. The die was cast. The feel of it changed something inside of him forever. As he walked holding the forbidden fruit in his hand, he found himself standing in the midst of a magnificent gale of olive trees which trapped wondrous prisms of light that turned every which way in a reflection of God's celestial glory. He peered into one of the prisms and savored a long, greedy look at himself.

He took a moment to languish in the admiration of his own stunning glory, and looked longer than he should have. His instinct was to look away, but he quickly became mesmerized with himself. The snare only deepened when momentarily he felt shamed by his self-directed abandon, but then, he paused to consider how truly marvelous and exceptional he was as a creation. Was he not the great cherub that covered? Who was like him in all of heaven? Who was wise like he? He was the fairest of ten thousand, brighter than the morning sun! He was Lucifer, Son of the Morning, the Covering Cherub. As he looked at himself and admired himself, he reveled in wonder at his own wonderful self.

While it is true that he legitimately tried to shake the preposterous train of thought, he became caught in a strange vortex of desire and self-adulation and decided to give himself leave to experience the nectar it provided. His newfound sense of self-love was overpowering, and at this point, he found himself intoxicated by its allure. For the very first time since the day he was created, he lifted his head in the air and involuntarily squared his chest. An embryonic, unclean spirit in the form of a fly found a place to nestle in the center of his heart. As it wedged itself in to ensure its own survival, Lucifer found himself deeply protective of it, much like a father to his firstborn son. In the days that followed, it would mature very quickly into an iniquity called pride.

The thought came to him that because of his anointing and splendor and just because of who he was, God's commandments did not apply to him. He was wrong…God is not a respecter of persons, and he makes no exceptions for sin. Lucifer decided to taste the fruit he held in his hand, just because he could. The idea sickened him at first—it was antithesis to his created nature. But the foulness of it passed and left only an uneasy feeling in its wake. Inadvertently, he turned to see if he were being watched.

All at once, and casting off restraint, he eagerly thrust the forbidden fruit he had been holding to the lips of his man-like face. He expected to find its juices pleasing to the palate, but instead, it was bitter once bitten and became rancid in the palm of his hand. Thrusting it away quickly, he turned once again to make sure no one was watching. How foolish it was of Jehoshua to forbid it, thought Lucifer. As food, it was wholly undesirable. It occurred to Lucifer, as the last clean and altogether wise thought he would eternally have, that when fruit is forbidden, it is not designed to be eaten.

Although he had been convinced that he was alone, from afar, many pairs of eyes had witnessed the entire heartbreaking spectacle. Where this garden now stood, there would one day be a full-scale war.

In a sweeping flourish that shattered the tranquility of the Garden, Lucifer gathered himself up in a blustering flurry and left the place he had once considered his retreat. He never looked back. That is when the changing first began. Something inside of him wanted to hide, but his newfound independence became an intoxicant. He felt naked but unashamed and with perverse abandon, sired a horde of new devils, among them sedition, witchcraft, heresy, self-will, and perversion. In an instant, his worship was turned into corruption. In the heavens, he would no more be called Lucifer, the Son of the Morning, but Adversary, Dragon,[5] the Prince of the Power of the Air, and the Devil. From henceforth, however, mankind would best know him as Satan, the Father of Lies.

Dunastes was there when he told the first one.[6]

The first time he'd heard Lucifer addressed by the title Beelzebul was actually just days before, and soon after he had polluted himself in the Garden. Several of Lucifer's top captains had been summoned for a meeting at Lucifer's throne on Earth, and Dunastes had gone along with them out of curiosity. He had not known then that it was a setup. He honored Lucifer greatly and wanted to make sure that his requirements were being sufficiently met by the militia. When he got there with the other captains, several angels of lower rank stood by, conversing with the great cherubim as if on familiar terms with him. This was most unusual, and for a moment stunned Dunastes. Lucifer turned too late to see his approach. Dunastes had already seen enough to set him on edge. Still, the other captains seemed unmoved by the uncharacteristic display of familiarity, and so, he relaxed, not wanting to cause offense to his revered prince.

As if that occurrence were not enough to raise suspicion, one of the captains who had been given the task of convincing Dunastes to come along, inadvertently addressed Lucifer by the odd and novel title. None of them had been created with subterfuge in their nature, and their slow descent into sedition rendered them amateurs in wickedness.

---

[5] Revelation 12:17
[6] John 8:44

"All hail, Lord Beelzebul!" cried Aruwm, as he knelt to render a salute.

He immediately realized his mistake and froze at attention. Although the slip was to prove a monumental blunder, it was given as a true display of allegiance. Aruwm had been one of the first to merchandise his spirit. The glaring look from Lucifer, in response to the slip, sent a large comet spinning out of orbit to rain dust and gases from its tail into the far reaches of the solar system. Dunastes stood speechless. His instincts were on fire.

Lucifer turned to his friend and top commander and gave a nod as a salute. Dunastes went down to one knee, with a fist to his breast, in the customary salute given to his prince, Lucifer. It also gave him time to quiet the commotion in his thoughts. As he came to a standing position, Dunastes met Lucifer's gaze with the steely demeanor of a soldier.

"Dunastes, my son and confidante," Lucifer started cautiously and trying to hide his agitation, "Is it well with you?"

Dunastes nodded without answering. He turned gently because he felt surrounded, and noticed that he was the leading character in the drama that was playing out before him. For a second, he regretted that he had not brought his gladius.

"Let my peace be upon you as dew, Commander Dunastes. You have both surprised us and alarmed us with your presence. To what do we owe this pleasure? I did not order you to come."

By now, Lucifer had recovered nicely, and honey was dripping from his lips. Lucifer was right, thought Dunastes, he had taken it upon himself to come. Not wishing to appear contentious, Dunastes tried to hide his unease.

"My Prince Lucifer, when Aruwm informed me of this meeting, I came out of my duty to you. The Armies of the Lord are at your disposal— it is my intention that every one of your requirements is carried out with dispatch. I trusted none other to come in my stead," replied the commander. Though all of this was spoken with sincerity, Dunastes touched the hilt of his pugio in secret and with restrained reassurance. He was created in the night but not last night, and being star-struck wasn't one of his frailties.

"I am the Son of the Morning, the Bright and Morning Star,"[7] cried Lucifer. He had turned from Dunastes and was now preaching to his rebellious choir. "Am I not seated at the right hand of Yahweh in majesty and power? I will exalt my throne above the heavens! I will ascend into heaven! I will ascend above the heavenly hosts! I will establish my dwelling on the Mountain of God in the sides of the North. I will ascend above the heights of the clouds. I am Beelzebul, the only begotten Son of God. I will be like the Most High!" cried Lucifer, a deceived orator on a self-constructed stage.

He was so full of himself that he was completely unaware that the deeper he descended into degradation, maggots, in the form of great serpents were eating away at the tabrets and pipes in his throat.

"All who are for me, fall down now and worship me, and you will reign with me for eternity!" cried Lucifer.

Incredulous, the sweeping proclamation caught Dunastes completely off-guard. The congregation, as if on signal, began to prostrate themselves before Lucifer's throne. It was a posture that the angelic hosts reserved for the Godhead only. Dunastes folded his arms across his chest to steady himself and to withstand the contamination. Not only was the worship of the cherubim rank with filth, the bold challenge to the Sonship of Jesus was the most convincing lie Satan would ever tell.

---

[7] Isaiah 14:13-16

Up till now, the concept of sin was an anomaly to Dunastes. The raw power of the spirit of rebellion not only confused the great commander, but momentarily weakened his resolve. He fled the scene in uncharacteristic anxiety to examine feelings he had never known before. It was the closest the resilient commander would ever come to waging his own personal battle with a devil called doubt. In the days that followed, inexplicably, he refused to speak of it even to Michael, and it was to prove his undoing. His silence on the matter of what he had observed would raise a question of his own allegiance. He would get his chance soon to make amends for this error in judgment, and give Lucifer and his angels a run for their money.

For now, here he stood sparring with God's top-ranking cherubim in full view of the elite of God's armies. It was not a good place to be. It was as wrong to openly challenge an officer, as it was to disobey a command. His plan required more time, but he knew then that he had all of the information he needed. Lucifer ended the duel by turning quickly and calling for Yibsam and his aides. The changing and the unexpected challenge from Dunastes had worn him down. He knew he needed added strength to move the plan to the next level.

"Yibsam!" Lucifer spat, "this commander has committed high treason before his prince and all of the armies of God. Disarm him at once!"

The order surprised the others, but as far as Dunastes was concerned, nothing could rival what he'd witnessed already.

"My Lord!" exclaimed Yibsam, "he has compatriots—it will start an insurrection."

Lucifer saw the irony in the statement and laughed out loud. Dunastes, who was unsure of the reason for Lucifer's laughter, was convinced that Lucifer had lost his mind.

Without so much as a signal, and to the shock of many, the mammoth front lines of the forward columns moved forward in sudden, full throttle in a hail of smoke, sound and fury. The lines then split in the middle, each moving at the speed of lightning around in parallel formation to each other to achieve a military flank called a double envelopment. The rippling pincer maneuver traveled all the way down the expanse, achieving a simultaneous flank to both rims of the outer lines. It was done with such a flawless execution, that the enemies stationed on the perimeters never knew what hit them. Those stationed in the inner cores were so discomfited by the precision of the tactic that when it was all over, they were still standing there in amazement fully mounted. The plot to flank the armies of God and rout them had just been outflanked.

Lucifer was momentarily blinded by the sheer genius of the counter attack, and did not see the great Archangel Michael until he was right upon them. Before any of them could recover from the blitzkrieg, Dunastes, Yibsam, and Lucifer were all surrounded by some of Dunastes' most indomitable senior officers. A regiment of captains, who had been positioned on the front lines all along, also rode up swiftly to take their positions beside Michael.

"Game over! Put them both in chains!" bellowed Prince Michael, "and gather all of the enemies of God that they may be proved."

Thinking that it was Lucifer and Yibsam of whom Michael gave the order, Dunastes was astonished when his own lieutenants, Otsmah, Shachah, and Sebazomai, stripped him of his crimson mantle, disarmed him of his pugio and gladius, and shackled him to Lucifer.

Chapter 3: Satan's Tail

A third of the heavenly host[8] had gone over to Lucifer's side. It was a number of staggering proportions. To understand how he did it is to understand the mystery of leaven.[9]

Lucifer was set to stand trial for treason on Mount Sion, the heavenly city of Jerusalem, even while his conspiracy was still underway. Dunastes was also slated to stand trial with him, named as one of the lead conspirators. As Michael's warriors had gathered thousands of ten thousands and thousands to probe their involvement in the rebellion, there were many like Dunastes whose allegiance was still in question. Though humiliated and deeply wounded by the indictment, in truth, Dunastes was more hurt that he had not been at the head of God's Armies when the extraordinary military coup had gone down.

Every time he thought on the degrading position in which he found himself, his sense of humiliation didn't last long. He would sit and replay the counter maneuver over and over again in his mind, savoring the absolute brilliance of the military action. A rival arch commander named Rhoomai had executed the brilliant charge and acted as chief commander at the head of Sabaoth. How Dunastes wished it had been him. This one had not been a war game; it had been the real thing, and he had missed out on it on the sidelines. Oh how that rankled him.

As he peered over at a sullen Lucifer whose prison was adjacent to his in the encampment, the plan he had begun to formulate earlier came back to him with renewed vigor. He'd overheard some of the top commanders say that Lucifer's plot was still underfoot, and that not all of the conspirators had been ferreted out. This was all Dunastes

---

[8] Revelation 12:3-4
[9] 1 Corinthians 5:6

needed to plan his next move, and it was a good thing for the commander, as well, that God sees and knows everything.

"Dunastes," whispered Lucifer, "is it well with you?"

Startled, Dunastes thought for a moment that Lucifer had perhaps overhead his thoughts. There had been no dialog whatever between them when they had been taken captive together. Dunastes was dragged along, overcome with shame, while the incisors in Lucifer's lion face dripped with rage. All along the columns, as they dragged him shackled and dishonored, the most devoted lieutenants of Dunastes lowered their heads in sorrow. He had been relieved of his command in such a publicly tragic fashion. The moment was heartbreaking even for his most stalwart warriors.

Never before since the moment of his creation, had Dunastes felt so disgraced and impotent. He would never rebel against the Most High God. The thought that his allegiance to Yahweh, the Living God, was now in doubt pierced his heart and caused him unspeakable grief. Michael knew him well, knew his heart, and was trusting that his tough, steely commander would move the next phase of the blitzkrieg into place out of sheer orneriness.

From inside of his cage, he answered warily, "It is well with me my prince, and you, Malak Yahweh, Prince Lucifer, is it well with you?"

In consideration of the circumstances, the salutation should have caused suspicion, but the spirit of pride in Lucifer had by now completely possessed him. His wisdom, now gone, was replaced by complete self-delusion.

"Does Dunastes serve God for naught? Curse him now and throw your allegiance to me!" spat Lucifer. "I have thousands times ten thousands who are poised to deliver me from this encampment. I need only give the word, and they will come. Throw your allegiance to me, Dunastes, and you shall reign with me in glory!"

Dunastes was glad that the makeshift prison walls separated them. He fought hard to cloak his contempt.

"Yes, my lord, and what a mighty fighting army your thousands times ten thousands proved themselves to be today. I think I had just enough time to blink before your ambush was ambushed. It's a good thing your ten thousands didn't put up too much of a fight when they were supplanted, or a speck of dust may have gotten into my eyes, and I would have missed the whole thing," bluffed the old commander. Dunastes knew he was pushing the envelope, but to score big, he knew he had to wager big.

"That is because, my comrade and commander, you were not at the head of my armies!" hissed Lucifer. "Throw your allegiance to me, Chief Commander Dunastes, and I will make you ruler up to the half of my kingdom," lied the tempter.

"You are mistaken, my lord, if you believe that a kingdom would suffice me," Dunastes replied with craftiness.

Lucifer paused to consider his words, and stepped right into the trap.

"Say on, Dunastes, I am listening," replied Lucifer, intrigued. Lucifer knew that winning the tough commander to his side would even the score considerably.

"Kingdoms are for kings, my lord, I am no king, but a soldier!" continued Dunastes. "I will see Prince Michael pay for what he has done to me this day! It is not a throne that I seek, but revenge!"

All around the prison walls, angelic sentries overhead the talk and smiled to themselves. Dunastes, the arch commander of the Lord's armies was in rare form even in captivity. Well into the night season, the two spoke at length and in whispers, as they planned and disagreed and planned some more.

At daybreak, Lucifer, Yibsam, and Dunastes were stirred from their chambers in chains and taken separately to different places. As they parted company, Lucifer eyed Dunastes knowingly, as Dunastes nodded to indicate his new allegiance. The commanders who had taken Dunastes walked with him quite a ways until they came to a place that was close to the Tabernacle of God. None but the righteous dared enter these grounds, and Dunastes was greatly humbled that he had been brought here. Why would he be brought here to the Mount of the Tabernacle if his loyalty were in doubt? What did this mean?

Just when Dunastes didn't think he could be surprised further, the commanders who had taken custody of him stepped back to part their ranks. Up through the midst walked Rhoomai, the arch commander who had led the counter attack the day before. "Come with me and do not speak," came the flat command from Rhoomai.

A perplexed Dunastes fell in behind him while the contingent of commanders brought up the rear. All at once, they got to a place at the ridge of a great valley and stopped. Rhoomai turned to face the top arch commander who was his absolute rival in war games. "I have something from Prince Michael that bears your signet," he said, as he nodded for one of his lieutenants to unshackle the great commander.

Dunastes' mouth dropped open as the lieutenant gave him the salute reserved for arch commanders and with a single swift motion, handed him his pugio. From his reaction, you would have thought he'd been handed the very scepter of God.

"Dunastes, whatever move you are planning," spoke Rhoomai with his eyes locked with the eyes of Dunastes, "plan it well and do not forget of whom your allegiance really belongs, my friend."

Dunastes was overcome with emotion. He grabbed Rhoomai by the arm and whispered, "Rhoomai! I worship the Most High Almighty and Living God, and it is to Him and Him only that my heart bows. I'm lost without Him! You make sure you tell my Commander, Malak Yahweh Michael that!"

Rhoomai nodded, clasping his hand over that of Dunastes, and moved swiftly to walk away.

Dunastes called after him, "Before this day is done, I will make amends for the notch that is missing from my dagger!"

Rhoomai turned to look once more upon his friend with a reserved smile and replied, "We're counting on it." With that, he was gone, leaving Dunastes to wonder at the strange turn of events. He was still the central character in a drama yet unfolding.

The night before and while he listened to Lucifer, Dunastes had been given a great prize—the opportunity to understand the mystery of iniquity. As he listened, he was baffled by the ease with which Lucifer had gained the cooperation of some of Michael's most able generals. They were assigned similar ranking as they were under Michael's command, as principalities[10] first, then powers secondarily, and then a maze of tertiary rulers under them. He was going to allow the greatest commanders of his militia to retain their dominion and rank, with the remainder of his cavalry and infantry comprised of lower ranking angels.

As Dunastes queried Lucifer to grasp the strength of his angels' allegiance, the genius of the rebellion was astounding. Like leaven, Lucifer's first act of treason in the Garden had become a deadly infection that he spread throughout the heavenly host. The power of one act, by one angel, had forever changed the Kingdom of God.

---

[10] Ephesians 6:12

When Lucifer left the Garden on the day he sinned in his heart, as was his habit, he started toward the temple of the Tabernacle of God where he spent most of his time in worship. When he got to the outer courts, something stopped him dead in his tracks. He stopped, momentarily mesmerized, by the grand symphony he heard coming from the inside.

He could hear harpers harping on golden harps, and the sound of praises like lightning, thunder, and voices all in unison shouting, "Holy, holy, holy, Lord God Almighty, which was, and is, and is to come! Thou art worthy, O Lord, to receive glory and honor and power; for thou hast created all things, and for thy pleasure they are and were created!" It was his custom to lead the worship of the four and twenty elders and the cherubim of the temple,[11] and for a still moment, he stood fixated to a strange inner wiring that tried to stir him to repentance. In the moment that he said no to the Spirit of God that was still in him, the die was cast forever. He bent himself toward destruction and made a deliberate decision that he would take some others with him.

He began to perpetuate the lie among his closest lieutenants that he, Lucifer, as the Son of the Morning, was in fact, the Son of God. He dared even to emphasize the postscript, the "only" begotten of the Father. On the strength of this single lie, he ensnared the hearts of those whose loyalty to him were strongest and drew the others in by watering the seedlings of deception, which had been cleverly grounded in logic. He mixed in just enough truth about the fact that he was there when the Godhead created the other angels, the heavens, and the earth to persuade them of his interconnected deity, and soon, they, too, were able to rehearse it in the ears of others to whom the iniquity was spreading.

The infantile fly that had originally nestled in Lucifer's bosom was now fully matured and in mating stage. As the defilement continued

---

[11] Revelation 4:8-11

throughout a third of the heavenly host, Lucifer infected them with unclean spirits that he sired out of his own power to create.

As the recruitment continued, Lucifer found that a crucial ingredient was to render them vile as soon as possible. Once they accepted his lies with conviction, their sanctification was rendered corrupted. The leaven had the effect of altering their righteous nature. He then demonized them by impregnating them with layers of unclean spirits so that the defilement would be irreversible. In the world to come, many of them would be responsible for doing the same thing to mankind; they just didn't know they would have to do it as disembodied spirits. They also didn't know that in the same way, they would soon be cast out of heaven, and they would perpetually roam the earth as trespassers and as legions of impure vagabonds, looking for somebody whom they could take possession of and call home.

The more powerful angels of Lucifer's kingdom were the principalities, powers, and rulers of nations. These would soon give mankind their greatest sorrow, but not without a valuable lesson from Dunastes, first.

Chapter 4: Above the Stars of Heaven

As Lucifer's outward metamorphosing changed him from cherub to devil, on the inside, he was just as defiled. Long gone were the tabrets, pipes, and jewels that were at one time so stunningly beautiful that they would have blinded human eyes.

He stood alone in an isolated place that looked like a great gilded cage and looked down briefly to study the monstrous great chain that encircled his waist and held his wrists in a vise. The immense, dull, and unadorned links of the chain curved around and around descending the length of his body to the soles of his feet, ending in massive brass rivets around his ankles. Every few seconds, he roared to show his displeasure.

The massive change in his appearance and his dark demeanor were so entirely opposite of his character, that one could but marvel at the spectacle he was making of himself. He was wholly and altogether defiled. To keep his pollution contained, Prince Michael had ordered him segregated and placed under the heavy guard of seraphim.[12] These were mammoth angels, of comparable strength and might as cherubim, with six wings, three faces, and eyes all about. They had been ordered not to address Lucifer, not to answer his queries, meet his demands, nor assist him in any way. What happened next can only be described as the devil's own personal sideshow.

He seemed not to understand that he had been taken captive and was about to be judged for his high treason. He began bellowing with the vocal chords he had left in his lion's face, "I am the Son of God, the Bright and Morning Star! I will exalt my throne above the heavens! I will be like the Most High God! I have my dwelling on the Mountain of God in the sides of the North! I am Beelzebul, the only

---

[12] Isaiah 6:2-6

34

Begotten of the Father! I will exalt my throne above the stars of the heavens!"

Screeching and stamping with the rage of a bull, he would yank the huge chain up and down and rake it across the iron bars of his cage. Then, twisting and thrusting himself all about, he would bend to build sufficient pressure in his loins and come up with an earth-shattering roar that could be heard in the Holy City. The seraphim that guarded him with flaming swords, glared at him without speaking, and this seemed to work him up in a greater frenzy.

As if his bellowing were not enough, he suddenly fell to the cage floor with the chain twisting in knots about his massive body. He began losing control, literally, and could best be described as going into seizures. The hemorrhaging taking place inside of him was tearing his insides out. He began rolling back and forth, spewing smoke, sulfur, and acidic fumes of putrefied waste into the air surrounding his cage. As he rolled from side to side in excruciating pain, he never saw the armies of seraphim and cherubim enter his chamber. Soon after, he was unceremoniously disbarred from heaven.

When he rebelled, he changed his purpose, and with his overthrow, came a change in his name. From henceforth, the cherub once known as Lucifer would become an enigma in heaven. On earth, so great a mystery would surround his beginning that the name that once meant brightness and beauty would eternally be associated with evil. He would no longer be known as Lucifer, the Son of the Morning, but Satan, the Adversary.

While Satan was making a spectacle of himself, his rank and file soldiers were having a bad day as well. His highest-ranking officers had been involved in the foray of the day before and were presently in segregation and under heavy guard. Dunastes had gathered the remainder of Satan's clandestine rebels in one of the most beautiful valleys of the earth realm. It was almost his undoing. As the angels continued to change from light to dark, from holy to unholy, their nature despised what they were created to worship.

The Northern Lights now bothered them, and the sun shone a little too bright. The fragrance of heaven became repugnant to them, and they began to shun the glory of the heavens. They now complained instead of worshipped, were suspicious instead of trusting, and discordant instead of cohesive. To Dunastes' dismay, they were a massive, rag tag bunch that lacked order and discipline and were a repulsive horde on top of that. Their change had not only been dramatic, but loathsome.

All it took to gain their allegiance was a show of Satan's signet ring. No one had dared question how it was that Dunastes had been freed, except Arubbah, the prince who had initially been given command of Lucifer's angels. Some had been in doubt about Dunastes because of what they'd heard of the fiasco of the day before, but seeing Satan's symbol of the leviathan in the hands of the commander seemed to quell their fears. Arubbah, who was still fuming over the demotion, challenged Dunastes's reason for gathering them in such a lovely place. But secretly, he also greatly distrusted the arch commander's real allegiance. Dunastes was as dyed in the wool to the cause of Almighty God as they came. Arubbah wondered to himself what had caused Prince Michael to even question his loyalty. Still, he couldn't deny the fact that the great arch commander had been dishonored before the entire Sabaoth.

"We are here to fight and not pick lilies, Commander! What a disagreeable place to assemble the armies of Beelzebul! Perhaps your enslavement has softened you," spat Arubbah.

Dunastes had to breathe slowly to keep from spitting at the foul being that stood before him. He had once been a brilliant and powerfully-built principality of heaven. Now, what stood before him was still big, but calculating and brooding. He had been a first lieutenant under Rhoomai's command and one of his more skilled tactical leaders. He was a logical choice to sit at the head of Lucifer's armies. As it were, Dunastes could not get over the shock that he had thrown his allegiance to Satan.

Dunastes started to trade barbs with him, and thought second of it. This one standing before him was treacherous, and it would not be wise to take him on as an opponent at this stage of the plan.

"Arubbah, do not agitate me today. Move your brigades into formation—see if you can teach them to look more like an army than their superiors performed on yesterday!" snapped the senior commander.

As Dunastes peered out over the multitude of fallen angels, he was intrigued by what he saw. They had to be herded into formation like quarrelsome cattle. Many of them were some of his most trusted fighters. It hurt deeply to know that they had thrown their allegiance. They knew, at a minimum, how to come attention, but you wouldn't have known it by observing them. It was then that Dunastes saw what he had not noticed before and immediately understood the reason for their feigned stupidity.

"Arubbah," he shouted, hoping that a change in command would not raise suspicion. "I want formations based on standards! Place the standard bearers at the head of each corp. I want leviathan in the front, unicorn in the second division, the lion in the third, the eagle in the rear guard, and so forth and so on."

As Dunastes gave the revised order, he turned quickly so that Arubbah would not be able to meet his gaze. He needed Arubbah to stay focused on his own personal resentment and not see things too clearly.

Arubbah turned to give the new command to newly-appointed captains under him, and once again, the massive corps of fallen angels dissembled into a foray of disorder and chaos. As the lines finally formed into what at least resembled an army, the standard bearers began to raise the crest of their standards high in the air. Dunastes smiled to himself; he was completely accurate in the assessment he had just made. His thought was that his quick thinking in issuing the revised command saved him from making a terrible blunder. What he did not know, but would soon learn, is that there is an aspect of blindness to evil that prevents the truth. To the pure all things are pure, but to the defiled, nothing is considered so pure that it cannot be polluted.

Arubbah and several of Satan's newest lieutenants rode up and down the lines, surveying and pressing for greater order. There was so much noise and movement throughout the ranks, that had Satan been there, he would have boiled with rage. Dunastes smiled to himself once again.

On the day before and just prior to the ambush, he had been captivated by the misarranged standards.

When he replayed the execution of the ambush in his mind, however, he realized later on that Rhoomai had tactically misarranged the standards as markers for himself. Because the columns had been so numerically massive, the standards helped him divide the corps so that he would know which division would move in what direction and under whose particular command once the counter-attack was underway. It was a brilliant device that only an arch commander would have even noticed.

Today, Dunastes misarranged the standards again for a different, but similar purpose. When he initially glanced toward the field of cavalrymen, he noticed that there were multitudes of angels whose brilliance were intense. The others, however, in fact the majority, had undergone unusual changes in their outward appearance. Some of the dirtied angels now had hard, blackened tortoise shells for breastplates, and their heads were devoid of hair. Their faces looked like masks of clay, and the whole bunch smelled like sulfur. To look upon them all at once, it was easy to pick out the pure angels of God.

But once Dunastes had them arranged by standards, he noticed that the pure ones were more evenly divided throughout the hosts as to not stick out so obviously. Still, he couldn't help but worry about two things: were they, like him, a part of the second blitzkrieg? And, to what extent had he rendered himself unclean as a result of his own subterfuge?

"What is the plan, Commander? We are in position and ready to fight!" Arubbah had to fight hard to show respect to Dunastes, but he was eager nonetheless to take the fight to the armies of God so that he could redeem himself.

Humph! Dunastes thought to himself. *You really think you are ready to fight? It took you half the morning to get them into straight lines. Is this what sin could do to a force of the best fighting angels anywhere? It had turned them into an inept pack of undisciplined and unruly misfits who stank to high heaven and held their swords like javelins.*

Whenever possible, the commander avoided meeting a direct gaze with any of the fallen angels. It was a distraction to him to not know what they thought of the glory of God, which was evident round about and upon him.

"Yes, Commander Arubbah, prince of the armies of Beelzebul, you have done well. Our lord, Beelzebub, will be pleased to get my report of your skill and efficiency in the field," lied Dunastes.

He was sure that he had just turned himself ten shades darker having said it. He then shared with Arubbah the plan he hoped would end this debacle for good. Upon hearing it, Arubbah was so impressed that just for a moment, he was glad that Dunastes had taken command.

As they moved the large columns of fallen angels out of the Earth valley and toward the Temple Mount in heaven, Dunastes signaled for Arubbah to change their formation once again. He ordered them to prepare for a pitched battle against the armies of God that would free Lucifer from his prison and lay siege on the Holy City. They would use a military formation called an echelon which required not only fighting agility, but precision—neither of which this army of fallen misfits possessed even on their best day.

Up and down the columns the captains over captains rode, guiding the corps of soldiers into a diagonal arrangement with one line set just behind the other and slightly off to the right. The effect was a ladder arrangement up and down the fighting field, which once one line was overtaken, the line behind it would step up as a reserve to prevent the success of another flanking strategy. As a final measure, and the one that would seal the maneuver, Dunastes strategically positioned all of the holy angels in the first wake of the echelon with all of the devils arranged behind them. He was careful to place the standard of the leviathan in the front line of the first wave as well.

Once the trap was set, he gave the command for the shophar to be sounded in Jerusalem, the City of God, and for all to go into battle yelling with the triumph of victory. It was a call to battle, and also the signal that Prince Michael was waiting for. Just hours before, the prisoners from the failed ambush had been released. Dunastes had met with them and placed them under Yibsam's directives. To say that they were hostile to him would be an understatement. Nonetheless, they had been apprised of his new allegiance to Beelzebul and had been given strict orders to submit to his command. Yibsam was suspicious of him from the start, but had met with Arubbah himself and knew that the lower ranking angels were being assembled for a pitched battle against Jerusalem.

The plan called for these better fighters under Yibsam's command to sweep down from their hiding place around the Temple Mount and encircle the armies of God, executing a military ploy called a pocket.

Dunastes would lead the charge from the other side, thereby isolating Michael's angels and setting them up for total annihilation.

At the sound of the shofar, a fetid smelling Yibsam now gave command for the commanders of Beelzebul to ready their swords for first strike.   Gone…was their brightness, their royalty, and great beauty.   Gone…was their agility, great wisdom, and splendor.   They had become little more than a rowdy multitude of high-ranking malcontents who bore no honor and cared little for the conventions of war.   It was all Yibsam could do to get them to make the assault at all. Still, they relished the thought of settling the score with Prince Michael.

As they moved in to follow the surprise plan attack from the rear, they could hear the thunderous roar of stallions and soldiers and expected to see the armies of God already engaged in battle with that of Dunastes' forces.   They were shocked, however, when they looked up to see Dunastes leading the attack with ten thousands of God's angels coming right at them with drawn swords and bearing the standard of leviathan, which symbolized Satan's regime.   Enraged at the betrayal of Dunastes, and thinking that he was actually leading the Sabaoth against them, they rushed head long without order or directive and never saw what hit them.

Wave after wave of the echelon of fallen angels struck their own comrades with such vehemence that it wasn't until they were all fallen that they were able to look back and fully perceive what had occurred. The demonic angels ambushed each other with terrible force and brutality, and the echelon formation proved especially destructive as each line in reserve slammed blindly into oncoming blades of their own brethren.   To deliver the final blow and to settle the issue, Rhoomai and a host of warriors used an encircling military tactic called a motitus to make sure no devil escaped the double edge of a gladdius. They, too, were unceremoniously expelled from heaven.

When it was over, Dunastes pulled out his pugio, and notched the hilt with his teeth.

Chapter 5: Gehenna

When Jesus, the only Begotten of the Father, found Dunastes, he was in the Tabernacle with his face to the floor and at the foot of the throne of God. The giant commander was so overcome with pent-up emotion that he had laid in this position without moving for more than two days.

"Dunastes," he heard the gentle but firm voice again, "is it well with you?"

In a haze, Dunastes lifted his chin. He thought he heard someone speak his name, but the glory of the place had so saturated his being that he felt engulfed by it. This moment and the events that were soon to unfold would make him a formidable foe of Satan forever.

"I needed to know what was inside of you, but I never for one moment doubted your allegiance."

This time, he heard the voice clearly and felt the hand on his shoulder of one so great that his name means, *"Who is like God?"*[13] It belonged to none other than Michael, the warring Archangel of God. He rarely smiled, but was capable of the deepest range of human sentiment and emotions.

As Jesus stood there grinning at Dunastes, Michael was his customarily humorless self. The Archangel[14] was created with the face and form of a human man, and did not belong to the order of angels known as cherubim or seraphim. He stood at more than fifteen feet in height, with an enormous wingspan reaching thirty-two feet from tip to tip. In recline, they arched more than three feet above his head and in length, stretched the full extent of his vast, powerful body.

---

[13] Daniel 12:1
[14] Jude 1:9

The eyes were the eyes of an eagle, the set jaw of chiseled marble; he appeared as one tinted in bronze. The hair was as black silk and cascaded into clusters of broad ribbons about his face and neck down to the shoulders. When he moved, the sweeping folds of a magnificent royal mantle cascaded in purple waves about his person. It was adorned with precious stones in hues of burning red and blue, with embroidered threads and fringed bells. The vestment was crisscrossed in folds of ivory and hues of burnt gold; his girdle was of fine linen, fastened about his waist in cords of purple. From the crown of his head to his feet, the intense glory of the Lord made him terrible to look upon.

Rhoomai, who stood beside Michael, stooped clumsily to extend a hand to the arch commander on the floor in order to assist him to his feet and momentarily lost his own grip. As the two commanders stumbled trying to steady the weight of the other, they both toppled to the floor in a heap. Jesus leaned back and roared with rich peals of laughter.

The warriors laughed as well, and even Michael couldn't resist the hilarity of it all. The unrestrained laughter brought welcomed relief. But just as suddenly as the laughter had erupted, it quieted. "Walk with me," was the still, solemn command that he gave to the high-ranking commanders. As Jesus grew silent and reflective, they deliberately adjusted their moods to match his. They walked through the lavish courts of the Temple interior without speaking and out to the Mount of the Tabernacle. As they walked, Jesus looked up and about as if seeing the unseen. Occasionally, he would stop altogether and tilt his head as though he were trying to catch a sound in the wind. He seemed to see and hear something they did not. But they did feel it— it was palpable.

The Lord paused to speak, "Because of what has happened here, one day, this heaven shall be rolled up like a scroll,[15] and it shall be

---

[15] Isaiah 34:4; Revelation 6:14-17

done away with forever. And in that day, there will be a new heaven and a new earth, and the throne of my Father shall be established forevermore."[16]

The Lord spoke the words with such conviction and fervor, that all three of the warriors were stunned by the pronouncement.

Dunastes could not imagine anything being built that could replace the beauty and splendor of the heaven of heavens.

"My Lord," he queried Jesus, eager to gain insight, "what has happened to Lucifer and to his cohorts? Will they be tried for treason? What of his throne in the Earth?"

At this, Jesus reached out, gripped his shoulder, and locked eyes with him. "I saw Satan fall like lightning.[17] I was there on Earth waiting when your gladiators deposed him. He is no longer to be called Lucifer, but Satan. The Earth is no more."

"My Lord," spoke the deep rumbling voice of an angelic champion named Chrioni—another of the arch commanders under Prince Michael.

All turned at once to face a commander with the heart of a lion. Even if you could pin him down, you were never guaranteed that he hadn't planned it that way. He was as big as Michael in height and girth and had the reputation of being one of the best swordsmen throughout the hosts. He had been there on the front lines with Dunastes when the final offensive had gone down. With a quick salute to all, he turned to Dunastes and lowered his head slightly in deference.

---

[16] Revelation 21:1-4
[17] Luke 10:18-20

"We are ready and anxious to do your bidding," Chrioni said, turning once more to address Jesus, as well as Prince Michael. "We have ten thousands times tens thousands fully mounted my Lord and awaiting your command to stomp the beaten enemy into fine dust. Our swords grow cold from idleness."

With that, Jesus thrust his head back, eyes shining and bright, and laughed until he almost cried. All of the commanders, save Michael, looked on, bewildered. Though the Son of God was a spirited opponent and a marksman that few felt daring enough to challenge, you would never have mistaken him for a soldier. For these angelic fighters, every context was conquest and tactic. For Jesus, every context was purpose. Michael never fully understood his perspective on things, but he loved him with all of his heart and being.

Dunastes, who had fully recovered by now, was shaking with anticipation at this latest announcement by Chrioni. He could hardly contain himself. He wondered momentarily if while he had been in worship he had by chance missed some of the action. Why were the armies of God being assembled? The thought of more real fighting—not just war games—made him clutch his chest the way a child would at the delivery of a long promised gift. At this, Jesus laughed even harder. The Son of God looked at each of them in turn and admired their strength and resolve. Their allegiance and obedience to the Father endeared them all the more to him.

"Today, commanders," he turned to look from one to the other, "we are not going to fight; we are going to assess. That, too, is a part of conquest."

"Prince Michael," Jesus addressed the Archangel now in a tone of seriousness, "you will brief Dunastes quickly so that we may leave within the hour. It will give you a moment more to explain some other things as well," Jesus stated it with a twinkle in his eye.

As yet, Dunastes had not been given any explanation for why he had been taken captive and chained in such a discreditable manner to Lucifer.

"Chrioni, you will make sure that Abaddon is prepared to show us Gehenna. I want to assess, as well as inspect," he stated solemnly.

"Rhoomai, I want a full report of the destruction that has been done to the celestial and atmospheric heavens and the Earth. We will recreate it not many days hence, and I want all of the hosts present as a witness to the manifold glory of the Father. All things shall be created for His good pleasure."

Jesus then turned and left them alone, knowing that they needed a time and space to relate to each other as the soldiers they were. He knew, better than they right now, that there was a battle between kingdoms that was still yet to come. He would need their craving for conquest and victory more now than ever, and there was a creature that had not yet been created that they must learn to revere and protect with this same craving. He and the Father had not yet figured out how to tell them this last part. They knew what Satan was going to do next and had prepared a bold plan that would always include the angelic garrisons as a crucial factor.

Later that day, they each found themselves on the precipice of the universe, gazing at the spectacle that had once been the most beautiful angel God had ever created. As they looked all about them, the devastation was at once terrible as it was breathtaking. What had once been lush, colorful, and idyllic, was now mangled like dark sewage. It boggled their minds—this kind of destruction was unknown to the angelic hosts.

They had been created in holiness, and it was all they had ever known. Sin and its aftermath had heretofore been unknown to them. Now, they, too, would be changed by it forever. Their way of life, of worship, of service, even of habitation, was irrevocably changed forever. Most of them would go on to accomplish great feats of victory, but not all of them. There was yet a group among them whose allegiance would fail with the creation of mankind, and who would commit a crime against God so heinous, that it would rival what Satan had done.

For now, they all looked long and hard at the former prince known as the Son of the Morning. He was rolling from side to side in the darkness with alternate cries of great pain and anguish. Sometimes, he would grow suddenly still, and at other times, he would jerk into odd positions as he wallowed on the ground. He seemed not to be able to sit or stand, and his limbs looked misshapen, even broken.

Prince Michael stood beside Jesus as Satan was observed, although the vanquished angel was blind to the great army that stood observing him, save the eyes of Jesus. Dunastes stood just to the rear of Michael, with the other arch commanders shoulder to shoulder with him. Their emotions ranged from astonishment to great sadness. There were many questions that filled their minds that would never be fully answered and only partially understood. One day, mankind would ask the same questions.

When Jesus had seen enough, he turned quickly and signaled for Michael to regather his brigades. In the darkness, the entire host was stunned by Satan's metamorphosing. When the change was finally done, all would look upon him and wonder that this was the man who had shaken the nations. But this was because they would never know from whence he had fallen.

All the while, the commanders standing beside him had been studying the face of Jesus. Lucifer had made the outrageous claim that he was the one who was the only begotten of the Father. They wondered how Jesus felt about the challenge to his deity. It wouldn't be the last time that Satan would put forth the peculiar and absurd claim. The next time it happened, it would be a bold affront to Jesus—

right to his face. It would take place in a wilderness on the third refurbished Earth, and Satan would lose that contest too.[18]

After they discharged the assembled army of God under Rhoomai's command, Dunastes and Chrioni were granted the privilege of accompanying Jesus and Prince Michael to view a newly-built habitation known only to them as Gehenna. To get to it, they traveled deep within the center of a tattered and shapeless Earth, but to a location that was closer to the surface than humans would ever realize. At the time these captains of the hosts first inspected it, it was shrouded in mystery even to those assigned the task of building it. What they were told right away was that it was a specially designed prison that would house the enemies of God. They assumed the reference was to Satan and his rebels. They were wrong on several accounts. Satan and his angels would soon be turned loose.[19]

Chrioni was the first to ask a question. "My Lord, is this to be the new abode of Satan and his angels until they are tried for high treason?"

There was a sad look on the face of Jesus[20] that none understood but Michael.

"It isn't designed to be a holding place, and none of its cursed inhabitants shall ever find it to be a place of rest,"[21] was the only explanation Jesus would offer at that point. His expression told them that they should ask no more questions. There seemed to be finality to what he had said.

"Come," Jesus said to them, "there is much to see."

---

[18] Matthew 4:1-10
[19] Revelation 20:3
[20] Jude 1:6
[21] 2 Peter 2:4; Matthew 15:30

As they sped quicker than the speed of light through the dark corridors and broken pillars of the shattered Earth, they got close enough to the outer perimeter of the massive structure to view its shape. The commanders were stunned to see that the abode called Gehenna both resembled and moved like that of a man's body. It seemed to move and reposition itself in perpetual motion as if it had a life energy all its own. They took note of the fact that it had a head, a torso, an expansive belly, and depths and depths of lower chambers that formed its legs and feet.

As they entered through its gates, they were first taken back by its ravenous and chameleon-like jaws that made an obnoxious sucking sound as they closed and opened relentlessly. The earsplitting sounds made by the sucking jaws and mouth sickened Dunastes, and momentarily, he wished he had not come. There was a shaft[22] leading into its mouth that connected the head to the belly, but they were first distracted by a dizzying vortex. It twisted around and around with perpetual motion and ran the breadth of its circumference—this, they took to be its throat. One day, it would trap its victims like the silk on a spider's web and repulse them with its terrors.[23]

Connecting the mouth to its dark belly was a monstrous, twisting thoroughfare known as the bottomless pit. It would forever be distinguished from Gehenna as the realm known as Abusos. While it descended deeply into the depths and caverns of hell, it went further beyond into even darker nether chambers and contained no bottom.

They moved deeper and deeper into the interior of Gehenna and what they saw was so visually staggering that not even the Lord would speak any words. The place seemed to elicit a reverent hush. Dunastes and Chrioni both realized at once why the Lord had said that it would not be a holding prison. This place, they could plainly see, in its vastness, was a chamber of horrors.

---

[22] Revelation 9:1-3
[23] Isaiah 5:14

Gehenna's inner cavity was made up of cages of varying depths and levels, and there seemed to be no permanent boundaries around them that one could describe as walls. The entire place seemed to have the ability to enlarge itself at will. Of equal consternation to them, were pitchy, reverberating sounds that seemed to have no origin. They were totally unfamiliar with these sounds and had nothing to relate them to. One day, they would come to recognize these as the sound of voices screaming in torment. For now, they only recognized them as unbearably pitiful and screeching noises. The sounds made the battle hardened angels cringe.

As they walked through the caverns of Gehenna, they noticed that there was no light here at all. That alone, evoked great terror. Only the glory of God about them provided the necessary light to see. Momentarily, Chrioni was intrigued by the sound that their feet made as they walked along and queried Jesus about it.

"My Lord, what is it that we walk on? The feel of it is unusual."

Without turning to look at him, Jesus replied, "It is a substance called brimstone."[24]

It was when they got to a region just beyond the main belly of Gehenna that they stopped dead in their tracks. The angels, as well as the Son of God, were completely disquieted by what they saw.

Before them, in cages of varying sizes and widths, were hordes of creatures so despicable, that their hissing, clawing, and spitting drove Michael, Dunastes, and Chrioni to draw their swords all at once. Dunastes thought harder on it and drew his pugio as well. The sights and sounds of the loathsome creatures caused them so much unease, that they refused to sheath their weapons until they were well on their way back to the heaven of heavens. Jesus looked at them and had to

---

[24] Revelation 19:20

stifle laughter. The thought came to him that here were angelic warriors who would fight...even in hell.

Anybody else would have had enough sense to be scared. He knew what they didn't—these creatures had been designed to torture anything with a soul or spirit. They had no idea what these creatures could do to a gladius. It was all he could do to keep from doubling over in laughter to see Dunastes standing there with a sword in one hand and his pugio in the other.

Abaddon,[25] the angel captain assigned to Gehenna, explained to them that upon its completion, these vile creatures would be turned loose to have their way with the inhabitants of this cursed underworld. The only missing elements, Abaddon explained, was the fire, the smoke, and the worms that never stopped their eating.[26]

There was yet one more place to be seen. Much further out, into an outer region of darkness, was a final place known as Tartarus. It was a greatly expansive abyss, filled with caverns of darkness, and yet, in character, was greatly different from Gehenna and Abusos. It was much quieter here, and there were no cages, but the angels looked on in bewilderment at the rows and rows of massive chains that were attached to the walls with iron rivets and shackles.[27] This chamber, too, would soon have its own horrors filled with the peculiar fiends that were created to torment the inhabitants of Gehenna.

The Lord was as anxious to end the tour, as the angelic warriors were to see light again. All remained silent as they moved swiftly up through each of the deadly regions.

When they got to the city of Jerusalem, Rhoomai joined them, and Prince Michael was the first to speak. He turned to Jesus first, who

---

[25] Revelation 9:11
[26] Mark 9:45-48
[27] 2 Peter 2:4

nodded approval, and then addressed the others. "Tomorrow, you will assemble the armies of Sabaoth with a special assignment. Satan will be taken first, under the command of Rhoomai's garrisons to Gehenna. He will be taken there, for a ...tour."

Prince Michael said it with effect, and Rhoomai smiled at what had been left unsaid but expected of him.

"After that," Michael continued, "he will be released."

The commanders were dumbfounded, but said nothing, awaiting further instruction from the commander of the Lord's hosts.

"Dunastes," Michael turned to the great commander and smiled at him, "you have done well, and there awaits you a very important assignment which we are convinced you will find most refreshing. For now, we need your garrisons, as well as that of Chrioni, Hatstalah, Sharath, and Towbunah to escort the angels of Satan into Gehenna as well. Make sure that they are given a thorough visit. Only Tartarus is off limits. You will then release them immediately. None of them is to be held captive there."

The commanders peered at him speechless, but were wholly obedient.

They looked from him to Jesus and saw that no matter how extraordinary the command appeared, there was something bigger at stake than their thoughts or wishes.

"Dunastes," Prince Michael finished, "I am placing Sabaoth under your command. You will report back to me once Satan and his armies are given their freedom. Is there a question?"

It was Chrioni, ever the one seeking understanding, who asked the question that no one else dared to ask. "My Lord," he addressed both

Jesus and Prince Michael, "will Satan and his cohorts ever be punished for their high treason against heaven?"

Jesus was the one who spoke. "Oh yes, but not now. One day, there will be war in heaven,[28] and all of you will get your moment to settle the score. There is something more that he is plotting, and we will wait until his judgment is full, and then, he will be tried and punished forever. Then, he, too, will have his place in the belly of hell for a time. After that, he will be released once more for a brief time to continue the course he has set for himself until we have had enough. Then, he and the enemies of God, which he has gathered unto himself, will be destroyed in a lake of fire that will burn for eternity.[29] There are some things yet to be revealed. The appointed time for all things is in my Father's hands only."

Prince Michael gave the final insight. "We want Satan and his devils to know what awaits them at the close of the age. We know that it is a great mystery to you now, but you will understand more by and by. Just as you felt terror by the darkness and wretchedness of Gehenna, so will he and his cohorts. As you lead Satan and his angels through its chambers and depths of terrors, you are to make sure that you inform them that it has been designed especially for them and shall be their future place of torment. From henceforth, you shall refer to it as Hell."

With that, Chrioni and Dunastes went to their knees in a salute and turned to leave quickly so that they could prepare their soldiers.

Dunastes had only one regret: He wished something could be added that would require the use of his pugio.

---

[28] Revelation 12:7-8
[29] Revelation 19:20; 20:14,15

Chapter 6: In the Beginning

In the beginning,[30] God created the heavens and the Earth. As he labored on each day of six days, all of the heavenly host looked on and shouted with a thunderous praise. Through his only begotten Son, the Word, who would one day be made flesh, God spoke forth light out of darkness, order out of chaos, and life out of death. There was a new being who was about to be created who would be given complete dominion over the restored Earth, as well as all of its inhabitants. This world and the hosts of it would be built to ensure and sustain his survival. Both the being and his companion would be called Man.

On the first day of his Creation, God called forth the light out of the darkness, and called the light Day, and the darkness, he called Night. That evening and the first morning would establish the first day. On the second day of his Creation, he separated the firmament that was in the midst of the mountains of chaotic, rushing waters from the firmament of the deep, creating a needed chasm. That evening and the second morning would establish the second day.

On the third day of his Creation, God spoke, and the firmament above the chasm was called heaven, and the waters below the chasm were gathered together in a heap so that the dry land could appear. Earth was the name that God gave to the dry land, and the gathering together of the waters under the firmament, he called seas. When he looked at what he had done, he saw that it was good. And God spoke, and the Earth brought forth grass, with herb-bearing seed of wheat, barley, oats, corn, and rice. After that, he created trees in abundance, with each tree bearing the fruit and seed after its own kind including the spruce, pine, evergreen, fur, and palm. When God looked, he saw that it was good, and the evening and the morning were the third day.

---

[30] Genesis 1

On the fourth day of his Creation, God spoke, and divided the lights of the firmament so that the day would be separated from the night. These lights would be for signs and for seasons, and for days and for years. There would be two great lights: the one to rule the day, and the lesser light to rule the night. Finally, he placed the stars to help rule the Earth by night, among them, Alula Borealis, Mimosa, Talitha, and Theta Aur. When he looked, he saw that everything was good, and the evening and morning were the fourth day.

On the fifth day, the waters below the firmament were now ready to support life. God spoke, and by his Word, the waters brought forth abundantly with great whales, jellyfish, the crocodile, dolphin, the salamander, the pickerel, octopus, and crab. With his breath, God created winged creatures and birds of every color and kind—among them, the eagle, the egret, meadowlark, robin, magpie, the woodpecker, seagull, toucan, and owl. These would fly in the firmament above the waters.

Then, God blessed them and said to them, "Be fruitful, multiply, and fill the waters and the heavens."

When God looked, he saw that it was good, and that evening and morning became the fifth day.

On the sixth day of Creation, God spoke and declared that the Earth would bring forth a great variety of living creatures: the gorilla, wildebeest, bobcat, bear, the ape, chinchilla, the marmot, the bison, and chamois, each after its own kind. Out of the dust of the Earth came forth a multitude of cattle and beast, including the tiger, kangaroo, antelope, lynx, the wolf, the alligator, coyote, and lion. And of every creeping thing, these included the scorpion, centipede, bees, the dragonfly, ant, butterfly, and beetle. Each was created after its own species and purpose. When God saw that there was order and that the Earth was ready to support the Man, he declared that all of it was good.

It was on the sixth day of Creation that God created the Man of earth, thereby making him mortal. He took handfuls of dirt and equal portions of water from the womb of the now fertile Earth, and squeezed and shaped the colored clay into a being he called Man. He started with a frame of delicate bones and vertebrae. He packed in muscles and connected it with sinews to give the form strength and resilience. The addition of two powerful engines—the brain and the heart—appeared to be what the creature needed to function as an independent being. He installed other organs, and with these, he added tissues and nerves that ran from head to foot. The angelic hosts watched with great joy as the Father worked his hand in and out of the compacted frame with moistened dirt from the Earth to give the figure definition and comeliness.

Once he was done with this, he stretched a thin membrane over the entire form and explained that it was skin. Into the being, he poured a thick rich substance, which he called blood, and added by way of explanation that the life of the creature would be in the blood. This creature called a Man was much like the angels in that he had the power to reason and the freedom to will. He would be a spirit, live in the corporal body fashioned of dirt and water, and have something called a soul. The angels of God stared in hushed astonishment. This being had been made in the very image of God, and he appeared to hold His likeness as well. They watched as God breathed his very Spirit into the nostrils of the Man, and thus, the Man became a living soul.

From a safe distance, Satan and his devils were watching too, but not in admiration. They were watching in total confusion. They could see the great joy and love that the Father used in creating the being. They also noted that the Man being seemed to be of an inferior nature than that of angels. He appeared to possess none of the power, strength, and authority of angels, but then too, there was something intriguing about the being that bothered Satan even then. It appeared that the spirit of the being connected him to God in a way that was different than for angels. He would think frequently back to this moment in time and remember his first sense of apprehension. But for now, he was already hatching another plot.

Everyone stood still waiting for the being to do something. But he didn't move an inch. He just seemed to stand there upright in a strange sort of paralysis. His form was powerful and muscular, but they noted that he had no wings with which to comport himself swiftly. His eyes were wide open, and his mouth was moving, but he made no sound and appeared to be blind. The glory of the Lord was strong about him, and the brightness of God's manifest presence served as his covering and adornment.

The Man being was surrounded by the entire heavenly host, including the secret horde of devils that watched from their hiding places. Their misshapen heads tilted one way and then the other as they peered on in interest, trying to figure out whether this creature could be a friend or foe. On their part, the angels of God watched trying to figure out how the being would manage to hold dominion over Satan's former habitation and his horde of devils. Although robust and of considerable height, the Man being appeared to be no match for the fallen angel and his cohorts.

All of a sudden, as if a key had been turned in an ignition, the Man took off running. The angels cheered loudly and laughed as he ran, and some even took off running with him. As a finished creation, he was vigorous and strong and had an agility that seemed more related to his corporal body. Even as he ran, the angels continued to inspect him to decide how the man was different from themselves. For one thing, they all noticed that he had parts that they did not. Even then, there was a group among them, which paid more attention to this latter fact than they should have.

Satan, for his part, did not care about the body parts as much as he cared about the fact that this being had succeeded him in being awarded authority and dominion over the Earth. He decided then and there that this being, made of Earth's dirt, was of no consequence to him and would be easy to usurp. It would be no time, he reasoned, before he would regain dominion over his throne. He was wrong about that. Man, with all of his complex internal wiring, would prove much more complicated to rule than the third who had thrown in their lot with him. That was, of course, the plan of God all along.

It was on the sixth day of Creation when God created the Man that he planted a garden eastward in Eden. Out of the ground and by His Word, God called forth trees of every variety and species. Some were lush with heavy fruit, while others were seed-bearing trees that were just pleasant to look upon. The very fingerprint of the Spirit of God could be seen throughout, in the pink encyclias, the yellow epidendrum, and orchards of Lady's slippers, the golden florets, and white asters. Each new species brought shouts of joy from the heavenly hosts, but then, all grew quiet when he created two more trees, strangely different from the rest.

Very few of those who were watching had been in the Mountain of God, and so, they had no way of knowing what Satan knew. He watched, dumbfounded, as God planted the Tree of Life, and then, the Tree of the Knowledge of Good and Evil[31] in the midst of his fallen kingdom. The move stirred a mixture of painful memories and sensations that all at once made him want to flee, but something seemed to root him to the ground in his hidden enclave.

Questions and speculations filled his mind at once. What could this mean, that God would plant these particular trees from the heaven of heavens under the care of the new being who was so much lower than the angels? Was he being taunted, as he had been by that wretched Rhoomai, when he was led as an observer through the chambers of hell? Again, the notion came to him to flee, but there was something mesmerizing about the whole scene playing out before him.

---

[31] Genesis 2:9

As Satan continued to watch the incredible design of the garden in Eden, he saw that God had placed a river there that would run through Eden to water the garden. From there, it parted into four main tributaries that compassed the whole of the Earth. The first was Pison that encircled the land of Havilah. It was a city filled with gold, bdellium, and onyx. The second was Gihon, which encompassed the land of Ethiopia, with the third called Hiddekel, just east of the land known as Assyria. The fourth main branch of the river came to be known as the great river Euphrates.[32]

The Lord God then took the Man and placed him in the garden to be its husbandman. His responsibility would be to tend and dress the garden and provide it a covering. As he spoke each commandment to the Man regarding his sphere of labor, he then spoke the words that Satan had once heard himself.

"Of every tree of the garden thou mayest freely eat," God said to the Man, "but of the Tree of the Knowledge of Good and Evil," God pointed as he spoke, "thou shall not eat of it at all."

The Man looked and listened, and nodded in obedience as he received the instruction. As he nodded, God continued, "For in the day that you eat thereof, you will surely die."

All looked on, including Dunastes, in awed silence. They didn't know what to think of what they were seeing or hearing, and they took special note of the affection that God seemed to have for this new and odd creature called Man.

As God walked and talked with the Man, communing with him on a level that was so different than with the angels, they all took note of how much of himself God placed in the Man.

---

[32] Genesis 2:11

God then communed with his Spirit and with the Word of his mouth, and said to all who were watching, "It is not good for the Man to be alone. I will make him a being who is like him and who is fit to be his companion."

The Man, as well as the great swell of witnesses, turned to the beasts and cattle that God had made, thinking that his reference was to one of these. God, knowing their thoughts and seeking to teach the Man his first lesson of dominion and authority, presented each beast, animal, and creeping thing so that he could name each one, and in so doing decide its purpose. When the Man was done, every witness took note of the fact that there was nothing fit to be the Man's companion. As for Satan, he was outraged by the entire sequence of events, but was then captivated by what God did next.

It was just before the close of the sixth day that God put the Man into a deep sleep. They watched in absolute wonder, as this state of the Man seemed to render him unconscious, yet fully functioning. The strange state that the Man was placed in by God seemed to render him vulnerable and helpless, and was so noted by all of the heavenly hosts. Inexplicably, God did not go back to the ground to make the Man's fit companion. Instead, he opened the cavity of the Man's torso and removed tissue and a portion of his ribs.

Using this bone and flesh, God worked with his hands to sculpt and give definition to the physical body of a second Man. This one, however, had soft curves where the first Man had been designed straight, flat, and muscular. This one was tender and lean, where the first one had been rugged and thick. This one was smaller and of a delicate frame, where the first had been broad-shouldered, wide-chested, and of tall stature. This one was wired differently on the interior, though both seemed to possess most of the same organs. This one had facial features that were exquisite and delicate. The forehead was narrower, and the cheekbones more defined. The lips were narrower, and the chin was very refined. Its torso was highly irregular, but pleasant to look upon, and all watched in incomprehension as God gave it something that the first Man did not have. That something was a womb. He used great care to sculpt it for the day that it would carry his own Son.

At first, there was just stunned silence. But then, the sound of such praise erupted throughout the heavens and the created worlds, that it shook the foundations of the Earth and settled it into home position. This new Man, with a womb, was God's crowning creation. Into her mouth, God blew his very breath and Spirit, and it became a living soul just as the first one before it. The angels adored this Man and knew intuitively that because of its great comeliness, it would always require their supernatural attention and care. Even then, Prince Michael, Prince Gabriel, and each of the arch commanders of Sabaoth realized that she would be the one that Satan would target first. Each instinctively touched the hilt of his sword, knowing that a new battle had just begun.

When God closed up the first Man, stood him upright, and awakened him, what stood waiting before him was like nothing he had seen among the fowl, the beasts, the cattle of the field, or the creeping things. As he stared at it, the blood rushed to his head, his mouth fell open, and he nearly fainted. His tongue wanted to say something, but it got twisted and felt heavy. Momentarily, he couldn't hear anything either, but God hit him in his head, and his senses recovered.

There were things happening to the rest of his body as well, but it would be a little while before he understood it all. Although God built this second Man with the understanding that she might very well be rejected, the heavens thundered with laughter when Adam found his tongue and declared the first covenant of marriage, "This is now bone of my bones, and flesh of my flesh!"

When God created the first and second Man, he named both of them Adam. The first one would be called a Man. The second would be called a Woman, because she was taken out of the Man. God wanted one species of Man, but two from one, and not two of the same.

God blessed them, and said to them, "Be fruitful and multiply and fill the whole Earth. Subdue it, and have dominion over it, including the fowl of the air, the fish of the sea, and every living creature that I have made for my purpose."

God continued, "Look, I have given you authority over every herb that bears seed and over every tree. You are free to eat of all of it as your meat."

God beheld everything that he had done and knew that it was good. The evening and the morning was the sixth day. On the seventh day, God blessed it and sanctified it, and rested from all of his labors—not because he was tired, but because he was finished.

Chapter 7: When Shiloh Comes

Before the serpent fell,[33] it was the most cunning and shrewd of all of the animals that God created. This is what got it into trouble with Satan.

"Is the Man, whom God has said will now rule over you and be your master, made of the same dirt as you?"

The other animals to which Satan presented the same question said nothing because his motive was very evident. The serpent, however, because he believed himself to be wise and astute, could not resist the theoretical debate.

"It is true that the Man is also made of the same earth as I, but God has commanded each of our species, including the Man, to be fruitful and to multiply and replenish the Earth. We have all been given the same commandment." Thinking that he could not be outwitted, the serpent added, "He differs from me only as a species."

Satan's retort came quick because he had planned the entire dialogue in advance. "If the Man is no different than you, except as a species, then why is he in dominance over you? Are you not wiser and subtler than any animal or beast that God has made? Why does God require the Man to have power over you?"

The knife was in, and at this point, Satan was just anchoring it. The serpent, however, was no fool and paused to rethink his position. At this point, it was still a game to him, but he seemed unaware of how high the stakes were growing.

As the serpent did not wish to appear unskillful in verbal contests, he just could not leave well enough alone. He replied with a slow,

---

[33] Genesis 3:1-14

unsure answer, "It is because he is made in the likeness and very image of God."

Again, Satan was quick to reply, "Are you saying that the Man, made of dirt, is like God?" Satan queried.

The serpent knew that he was caught, but his cunning left no room for surrender. He caught the insinuation that if the Man was like God, and he was made of the same dirt as the serpent, then he, too, must be just like God.

Smelling blood, Satan moved in for the kill. "It is not just for the Man to have dominion over you. He has not earned the right and should be made to prove that he is the most fit to rule. There is no difference between you and the Man. I believe the Man to be inferior to you. Look at how the Woman affects him." Satan paused with this to watch the serpent's reaction. He could see that the serpent was weighing the logic and was no longer sparring with him.

He continued, "There is a way to show God that you are just as capable as the Man of having dominion over all of the Earth."

The serpent's distrust was now gone. Initially, he, too, doubted the motive of Satan, but he found himself seeing the good logic of the fallen angel.

What Satan had said was true in every respect, reasoned the serpent. If he could show God that that the Man was not as wise as he and could be too easily influenced by the Woman, then God would see that he, the serpent, was a better choice to rule.

It was not easy to get the serpent to go along with the plan, but they both agreed that the Woman should be the one that the serpent should approach first. Secretly, they both envied the fact that the angels loved her so. Not only that, but the Woman had a womb which they understood could carry the seed of the Man to produce a whole race of men. If they were to stop the Man from filling the Earth with his own kind and thus controlling the fate of all of the other created animals and beasts, then they could usurp his authority and rule the Earth themselves.

It was the Woman that they had to lead in rebellion to God, they knew. They had observed the Man closely and could see that he was slow to reason things out, and even then, he seemed to want to have more answers before he would commit to a decision. Could this be the highly intelligent being that God had given rule over his creation? The Woman seemed given more to her instincts, and they could see the sway she held over the Man's thinking. They also took note of the fact that the Woman's great loveliness disposed her toward vanity, and they were interested to see how they could play this to their advantage. If they could get her to eat of the tree that God had forbidden, they felt certain that she would give the fruit to the Man as well. The Man, they reasoned, would follow the Woman in order to please her. He seemed somehow vulnerable whenever she was around and appeared to soften when she touched him.

Gaining the serpent's allegiance was easier than Satan expected. He would fill the serpent's heart and speak with the serpent's lips and be the power behind the enticement. The serpent, being a willing ally, could never know that with his fall, would come the fall of every animal, beast, and creature as well. The man would go on to dominate the Earth to the point of pollution. And, as a result of the entrance of sin, one day he would hunt many animals and beasts to extinction.

In the realm of the spirit, Dunastes and a great garrison of angelic warriors had witnessed the entire exchange. Although the serpent was able to clearly see them there, there was a great gulf fixed between the two realms so that they could not intervene to stop the great catastrophe that was about to play out in the most beautiful garden imaginable. It was the one thing that God had changed about the creation of the new Earth that most perplexed the heavenly host. The laws of intervention, which now governed the Earth and its inhabitants, were different from the laws that governed the heavens. There were certain things they could do only with permission from God and other things that were forbidden altogether.

With bated breath, the garrisons of angels watched the approach of the serpent to the Woman and the Man and were helpless to reveal the plot that they had just overhead. None but the heavenly hosts could see that Satan had taken full possession of the serpent's body. As Satan moved ahead boldly with his plan, the arch commander Dunastes, who was a sworn enemy of Satan's, began making a plan of his own.

"Yea, has God said that there are trees in the Garden of Eden that you may not eat from?"

The Woman who was laughing and flirting with the Man, who stood close by, turned to look at the serpent. It stood as tall as a man in height, and with its great aplomb and dignity, was clearly one of the most intellectual and beautiful of the living creatures. The wings were so broad, colorful, and full that they gave the serpent an added appearance of grandeur. This seemed to generate a certain immodesty in the serpent's bearing, and it developed the habit of flexing its wings just for the effect it gave. Layers and layers of fine feathers covered the bulk of its upper torso, and the skin of its backside and legs were supple and tender.

"We may eat of each of the trees in the Garden,"[34] replied the Woman to the serpent, "except for the one that stands in the center of the Garden. God told us that we are not to eat the fruit of that particular tree, and that we are not to touch it."

Although she added her own words to what God said, had she stopped there, she would have been safe. Thinking that she needed to further explain so as not to make God's command seem unreasonable,

---

[34] Genesis 3:2-4

67

she added, "He has warned us that the fruit of this tree can cause certain death."

At this point, the Man became curious and drew near to hear what the serpent was saying. He knew that the serpent was not a favorite of the Woman and wondered that the serpent would try to converse with her.

"He did not really mean that you would die," said the serpent coyly.

He placed a greater emphasis on the word "die" when he spoke it so that the Woman would feel that the notion was a foolish one. The Man was outraged by the serpent's words and saw the trick immediately. As he moved to stand between the Woman and the serpent, he meant the gesture to challenge the serpent, but it had no affect, and the serpent continued its dialogue.

"God knows that on the day that you eat the fruit of that particular tree, both you and the Man will be able to see things that are now invisible to you in the spirit realm, and you shall have the same ability as He to know the difference between good and evil."

The Woman was caught immediately. It made sense to her that if the tree with such lovely fruit was in the Garden, that the fruit should be available to eat the same as all of the other trees. The serpent was known to be very wise, and she was immediately flattered that it would take the effort to address her rather than the Man. She believed the serpent that if, by eating the fruit of the tree, it would make her wise like the serpent was wise, it would be a very good thing for all concerned.

The serpent turned first and started walking to the tree. The Man stepped forward and blocked the way of the Woman to follow the serpent, but before he could address the serpent, she had stepped out from behind him and gone ahead to walk beside the serpent. This greatly annoyed the Man, but he kept his silence. He did not believe that the Woman would actually partake of the forbidden fruit. He thought that this was just a game.

When the serpent got to the tree, it snatched one of the fruit hanging closest to them and thrust it toward the Woman's nose and mouth. Ensnared, the Woman stopped to catch its fragrance and because of the words of the tempter, added elements to the forbidden fruit that the serpent had not even suggested. The deception was complete, when she took the fruit from the serpent's hand and held it in her own. She then turned to the Man with a smile, and the tempted became a temptress.

Playfully, she skipped about the Tree of the Knowledge of Good and Evil with the fruit dangling from her hands as if in one moment she would eat it, and in the next, she would not. She tossed it back and forth to the serpent laughing as she did. The serpent would laugh and toss it back to her in order to increase her comfort with disobeying God. The Man did not like the game, but his attention was riveted in the wrong direction. His eyes were on the serpent, but they should have been on his wife.

As if on a dare from the serpent, the Woman suddenly thrust it to her mouth and bit deeply into its core. She was determined to show the serpent that she would eat the fruit of her own accord, and not because of anything he had said. When he noticed that his Woman had bitten the fruit forbidden by God, the Man was overtaken with a terror heretofore unknown to him. What had the Woman done? How could it be undone? The Man's heart began to pound with such strength, that he feared it would come out of his chest.

As the Woman held the fruit out for the Man to eat of it as well, he backed up and started to flee. She could see that the fun and games were over. And then, all at once, another emotion hit the Man that was equally foreign to him. It was anger…but it was not directed at the serpent. He turned to the Woman, and she could see his displeasure immediately.

"What is this that you have done?" demanded the Man to the Woman. "We will surely die. God has said so."

The Woman was immediately injured by the sharpness of her husband's rebuke. "No, you are wrong; see, I am still alive. There is no harm to eat. It will make you wise like the serpent."

The Man studied her carefully with both sadness and regret. He loved the Woman and did not want to see her die. It would mean that he would be alone without her. Whatever fate awaited the Woman, he knew that he loved her too much to let her face it alone. As she stood holding the fruit out for the Man, the Man took of it and ate it from the Woman's hand.

Just before they first looked at themselves, the serpent turned to flee. He was able to get just a few feet in distance before Dunastes caught him by the throat. He lifted his pugio high for the serpent to see, and then ordered several of his lieutenants to put him in chains.

"What is that to me?" spat the serpent, "the Man has fallen, and will soon die. Now the dominion of the Earth belongs to me."

Dunastes peered at the serpent with a sly grin, "True, but once the Lord judges you for what you have done this day, your hide belongs to me!" With that, Dunastes turned swiftly to return to the throne of God for further orders.

The consequence of sin was not quick; it actually caught the Man and the Woman unaware. As they stood embroiled in an odd exchange of blame, it was the Woman who first noticed that their skin was bare. All of the other animals in nature had feathers, fur, wings, or scales. They seemed to have very little to cover themselves, she noticed, and what little they had didn't seem adequate to cover what needed to be hidden from the eyes of the animals and other spirit beings that seemed to surround them constantly.

The Man was slower to notice his own bare genitals, but just as his wife first became self-conscious of her bare genital parts, he noticed that his were bare as well. Not only that, but until that very moment, he had been able to see her nakedness without distraction, but now, it seemed that he could not. The most peculiar sensation of shame overtook them both, and neither was aware of the connection it had with their act of disobedience. They kept waiting to die, and as nothing happened, the anger between them subsided.

As the fruit began to take its full effect, their eyes came completely open. The sense of shame was replaced by condemnation, and they sought a safe place to hide from God. They hoped that perhaps God would not find out, so they tried to cover their guilt with aprons of fig leaves.

"Adam!" It was the Voice of God.

They both heard the Voice walking in the Garden of Eden during the cool hours of dusk when the Earth was most beautiful.

"Why are you hidden from me?"

The Man caught his wife by the hand, and haltingly, they came out from behind their hiding place in the trees.

The Man spoke first, "I heard your Voice in the Garden, and it made me afraid, and because I am naked, I thought it good to cover myself, and that is why I hid."

The Lord peered at their flimsy attempt to make girdles out of leaves.

"Who told you that you were naked?" queried the Lord without a show of emotion.

Adam responded to the Voice with a mixture of dread, dishonor, and hopelessness. In the last few hours of his life, he had experienced every single emotion that mankind would ever know. At this moment, though, when he had to give an account to God for his disobedience, the feeling of aloneness nearly overwhelmed him.

"Did you eat from the tree that I told you not to eat of?" The Voice was now a bit thicker.

Adam, on his part, was now past a sense of remorse and was now on to blame. He lifted his head to the Voice, now a bit more boldly, and replied, "The Woman whom you gave to me because you said I needed a helper—she is the one who first ate of the fruit, and then, she gave it to me to eat as well."

At this, the Woman beside him hung her head and wept the first tears of a woman. It hurt her deeply and gave birth to a need in a woman to feel safe with a man.

With the Man's abdication of responsibility, the Voice of the Lord now turned to the Woman. "What have you done?" the Voice demanded of her.

She, with fresh flowing tears, readily admitted her guilt. "I did it. It was the serpent who tricked me into disobeying you."

As they both stood partially naked before the Voice, they fully expected to die. In fact, they each longed for it, thinking that it would somehow pay the price of their disobedience, thus allowing their generations another chance.

The effects of the fruit that they had eaten from the Tree of the Knowledge of Good and Evil continued to work its full effect. As if their agony were not enough, they both seemed to understand the gravity of their act all at once. As the bite of the forbidden fruit worked itself into the consciousness of their souls, they gained extensive knowledge of the great destruction that their act of disobedience would bring to all animals and beasts, the vegetation of the field, and the great beauty and sanctity of the Earth. They had from henceforth and forever introduced the Earth and all of its inhabitants to the ravages of sin.

As the knowledge of the impact of what they had done began to overburden them, they fell to the ground before the Voice and wept in tremendous agony. Out of mercy, the Lord would not let them see what the generations of their sons and daughters would experience in untold sickness, poverty, disease, and death. But in just a little while, they would have to face Satan on their own…and he would show neither them nor their generations any mercy, ever.

When the Voice suddenly redirected to the serpent that had been dragged into the Garden in chains just minutes before, they could also see Satan clearly. He was standing there with the serpent and was also in chains. God turned to address the serpent first.

"Because of what you have done, you will be more cursed than any animal, beast, or living creature I have ever made. From henceforth, and because of your curse, you will wallow on your belly in order to transport yourself, and when you eat, you will be forced to swallow mouthfuls of dirt along with your food. Dunastes, take him and do with him as you have requested!"

The sound of the Lord's Voice had been dreadful to hear, and the appearance of the Earth at the sound of His fury was as it were before a great tornado is about to strike.

Next, the Voice turned to Satan who now stood apart from the serpent. He was about to turn an insolent glance at the Man and the Woman when a glint of light caught his attention to the right of where he stood. He turned at that moment to see the angel Dunastes slash the serpent with his pugio. The serpent screeched and groveled in agony as the angel flayed the skin from his body. The blood from the animal flowed in torrents, and his form began to change with each fresh cut. As it writhed in agony on the ground, it seemed to twist itself round and round into a long tube-like shape. Where there had once been feet, wings, and arms, now there was nothing. Just before Satan heard God call him by name, he turned once more to see Dunastes strike the serpent in the mouth. From his throat came a hissing sound instead of speech, and his tongue was now split like a fork.

"As for you, Satan, I will put an intense hatred and war between your kingdom and my Son's Kingdom. His Kingdom will bruise your head, but your kingdom will only bruise his heel."

Satan glared in a dark rage, not understanding the full revelation of the words of God. What he did understand, however, was that his fight was now with the seed of the Woman, which would come to be known as the Church.

The Voice then redirected to the Woman. "I will greatly multiply your tears and sorrow as a Woman, and when you bring forth children of your womb, your suffering will be multiplied. From now on, you are subject to your husband's headship, and he will always seek to use his position to maintain rulership over you."

The first thought of the Woman after hearing this last judgment from God was that indeed this would be death.

Finally, the Voice redirected to the Man. "Because you made the choice to disobey me and to hearken to the voice of your wife, and because you ate of the tree that I specifically told you not to, the soil of the Earth is now cursed specifically for the sake of making your judgment full. As you till it for your meat, it will forever bring you thorns and thistles. In the sweat of your brow, you will labor for bread until the moment of your death. For out of the soil I created you, and back to the soil you shall return at your death."

When the Voice of the Lord grew silent, the sun went down on the Man and the Woman as they stood now separated from God.

With the skins of the serpent, the Lord dressed the Man and his wife and drove them forth from the Garden of Eden. Cherubim were posted at the east of the Garden of Eden to stop the Man and his wife named Eve from ever entering the Garden again.[35] The Lord knew that if they partook of the fruit of the Tree of Life, having lost their innocence, they would now live forever in their fallen state.

As the heavenly host stood watching as the Man led his wife forth out of the Garden, Dunastes turned and couldn't help asking when things would be made whole again.

"When Shiloh comes…" was the reply he heard but would never fully comprehend no matter how much he looked into it.

---

[35] Genesis 3:22-24

Chapter 8: Strange Fruit

When God destroyed the Earth by flood, it was mainly because of a deed so heinous, that it forced him to start all over again. True to form, Satan was behind it.

Soon after the fall of man, there was a population explosion across the globe. But as man multiplied in numbers, so did sin and corruption. There was such an increase in wickedness, that there was scarcely a righteous man to be found anywhere on the Earth. Brother rose against brother. Tribes of families declared battle lines against other tribes. The increase in murder, violence, deception, and mayhem affected every living thing created. Even the Earth groaned, anxiously awaiting its own deliverance.

Perhaps, then, it is not a surprise that the heavenly host were affected as well.

"Where have you been?" demanded Dunastes of one of his closest lieutenants named Makbar, whose name meant Covering.

Several of the commander's top aides had been missing in action for several of the war games. They were some of his most noble officers, and it was uncharacteristic of them to disobey a direct command. Angels were wired to obey.

Makbar was unaffected by the challenge and met his commander's steely gaze. "I have been busy on the Earth realm, my lord, and have been unable to keep my charge," stated the angelic captain in an unapologetic tone. But there was something about his demeanor and his eyes that bothered the seasoned top commander.

"You have been busy doing what?" demanded Dunastes.

"My lord, I am under direct orders from Prince Michael, and I am unable to give more details." Makbar lifted his chin in defiance, and for a moment, Dunastes considered putting him in chains.

Dunastes could see that Makbar's manner was a ruse, but was intrigued by the flagrant impudence of his lieutenant. This was not the manner of Makbar, and the transformation greatly affected Dunastes.

"Makbar," Dunastes changed his tone to that of an appeal, "What is it? What is the cause for your contempt today?"

Momentarily, Makbar looked away, melting under the conciliatory tone of the commander whom he greatly loved and admired. He could not meet the commander's eyes at this point because he was afraid that his terrible secret[36] would be too quickly exposed.

Dunastes circled the lieutenant to his right, causing the underling great discomfort. As he moved slowly peering at Makbar from the back of his torso, it was the first time that he noticed the garment. Instead of the traditional mantel required of militia, Makbar wore a beautiful tunic of Earth's design and adornment. Dunastes was momentarily bothered that he had not noticed it at first. As the commander peered down to his footwear, he noticed that Makbar wore sandals that were indicative of mankind's invention. As he kept circling his lieutenant to inspect his outerwear, he was dismayed to see that his warrior was missing his weapon. From the perspective of one as militarily focused as Dunastes, it was like looking at a naked angel.

"Lieutenant!" cried the commander, "where is your weapon?"

Dunastes had by now made it back around to the face of the angel, having fully inspected him from all angles. Makbar looked up to meet the eyes of the commander, but then looked down quickly, saying nothing. This kind of avoidance from such a strong, rugged fighter as

---

[36] Genesis 6:1-4

Makbar spoke volumes. Dunastes tried to calm himself. He needed answers and did not want to intimidate his aide to silence. He wanted him to speak and to assure him that this was all a mistake. He wanted Makbar to provide some solid explanation that made sense to him, so that all would be forgiven. Instead, Makbar stood before him in silence with cast-down eyes and a heavy heart.

The silence was oppressive, and was finally broken by the approach of arch commander, Chrioni.

"Makbar, I assume you are having trouble explaining your absences?" started Chrioni.

Dunastes looked from Makbar to Chrioni, hoping that Chrioni could provide some insight. Makbar was a trusted lieutenant, and of all of his closest captains, he would have been the one whom Dunastes would look to first with the most difficult of assignments. Dunastes could see that Chrioni was greatly agitated and stepped back, hoping that he was the one who could get some information out of Makbar.

"My lord, I have nothing to say," replied Makbar, this time to Chrioni.

"Well, tell me, lieutenant, since you have nothing to say, who is the Earth woman whose adornment you wear?" Chrioni spat the statement out through his teeth, and Dunastes could see that he was struggling to maintain his composure.

A woman! Dunastes peered at his colleague wondering where this questioning was coming from.

Makbar looked up at the commander once again in defiance.

"What is that to you?" Makbar demanded, this time meeting the gaze of the commander, eye to eye.

Both Chrioni and Dunastes moved a step toward the defiant lieutenant at once. It was then that Makbar realized he had no weapon, but both of the commanders caught the slight move of his arm to his side where his side arm would typically have been.

"You dare take a weapon to your commander, Makbar?" Dunastes demanded in a fit of a rage.

"I have no weapon, my lord," was the flat reply from the lieutenant.

This time, Chrioni raised his arm for Dunastes to stand down. He moved even closer to Makbar, almost nose to nose, and began the circling motion that Dunastes had just done. He, too, looked up and down the angelic warrior, but without the surprise. When he once again faced Makbar, he stepped back and spoke to Dunastes as if the lieutenant was not even standing there.

"I have ordered several of my aides placed in chains, and I advise you to do the same with this one until we can get to the bottom of their treachery." Chrioni spoke it with authority and left both Makbar and Dunastes in the silence with which he first approached. Makbar once again cast his eyes downward.

Dunastes circled him to the right once more and decided to make one final appeal. "Makbar! Assure your commander that there is some mistake. Why have you been missing from the war games, and why are you dressed in this disorderly manner?" Again, Dunastes' tone was deliberately conciliatory.

Makbar said nothing, just staring at some invisible target on the breastplate of the tough commander before him.

"Very well, Makbar, you have decided your own fate. Until you are ready to give a reason for your insubordination, you will languish in chains until I am able to gain some intelligence about what you and the others have been up to." Dunastes turned and signaled for three of his lieutenants to come.

"Put Makbar in chains!" demanded Dunastes.

The three lieutenants stared at him in disbelief, wanting to make sure that they had heard him correctly.

In a quieter tone, Dunastes said it again. "Put Makbar in chains; he is under arrest for subversion."

With that, Dunastes turned and walked away with a mixture of emotions. He would get to the bottom of this matter about some woman, and the thought came to him that Satan had better not have anything to do with it.

Later that evening as Makbar sat with several others in a common jail, he came to regret his earlier show of defiance. Although he loved the woman, his allegiance to Arch Commander Dunastes was not less, but stronger. He wrestled with emotions that were both novel and perplexing, and when he was done weighing one option against another, he made a fateful decision that would cost him his habitation with God and the holy angels. He decided he would join the many others like him who had thrown in their lot with the women of the Earth and with mankind. If there were any misgiving that continued to plague his mind, it was the unspeakable thought that his decision could mean a blow against God in favor of Satan. Oh, how he wished there was some other way he could do this thing, for he hated Satan with everything inside of him. But his mind was made up. He had to have the woman.

At the same moment that Makbar sealed his own fate with a decision that would cost him more than he could know, Dunastes stood with the other arch commanders listening to a strange tale from the lips of Satan himself. They were all standing in the temple court at God's throne, listening to the Devil make a shameful accusation against the hosts of heaven. It all started, he said, when a garrison of Earth soldiers moved against a small village and slaughtered the men and small children. They set the small enclave on fire and took livestock, hidden gold, and other valued treasures, but the women were saved alive and taken hostage. Satan's devils had been there to direct the carnage, and the powers of darkness which ruled that region had successfully moved the conflict to a boiling point.

When the Earth soldiers got their fill of debauchery and wine, they then took the women and young girls and raped them repeatedly in gangs. When they were done with their violence and mayhem, they put the women out of their misery by beheading each one with their swords. As Satan described the scene with melodrama and a good dose of embellishment, he would turn to look into the eyes of the arch commanders, knowing how the tale would greatly affect them. He then went on to describe how the angels of God had stood watching the scene, unable by the laws of heaven to intervene. This scene had played out many times before them, but for some inexplicable reason, this time had been too much.

He told of how some of them had broken the laws of heaven by later killing the guilty soldiers, which was true, but then lied by saying the angels had killed other men who had not even been involved in the massacre. Satan lied by stating that the angels had taken an oath not to allow men to ever abuse women again, but then spoke a little truth when he said many of them had their favorite women whom they were particularly protective of. With an exaggerated air of self-importance, he lied and stated that there had been wide-spread fornication of legions of God's angels with women, and that God's arch commanders had long known of it and done nothing to check its spread.

At this, Prince Michael glared at his arch commanders who were so angry that they advanced toward Satan and disrespectfully drew their swords before the throne of God.

"Do you dare draw your weapons before the presence of Yahweh?" demanded Michael.

His voice thundered through the temple grounds.

"Drop your weapons at once!" bellowed the Archangel.

All of the arch commanders dropped their weapons before the throne and fell on their faces before God. But on God's part, He kind of wished they had cut Satan first and then done homage. Had the arch commanders known the mind of God, they would gladly have obliged.

The Lord signaled for the commanders to stand to their feet, while Michael turned his displeasure to Satan who enjoyed being the center of attention. At a nod from God, Satan continued his tale. At first, Satan explained, the plan in the hosts was just to protect the women from the heightened incidence of rapes and murder by men. But then, he explained, their feelings began to twist. He admitted to talking to many of them on several occasions, to test their affection for the women to see if it was pure. He claimed that as he tested their motives for wanting to protect the women more than men, he found that many of them would speak in terms of endearment that he found offensive to their estate. He then lied to God and stated that this was all of the information he had. What he left out was the continual verbal assault his devils made on the conscience of the angels.

With a flourish, Satan finished his lengthy lies and half-truths, by declaring himself innocent of any wrongdoing and just a messenger of the truth.

God dismissed him from the temple and nodded for Michael to send one of his aides to call for an angel named Chamad, whose name meant Delight. During the interim, one arch commander after the other stepped forward to give a report to God of missing angels from their ranks. Of those who were missing, some were not all soldiers. Some were messengers, others were guardians, and still others were ministers. Each commander reported out the names, ranks, and growing number of those missing. Each commander's report staggered the mind of Dunastes. He couldn't believe that this had been underfoot, and that he had not noticed it. While it was true that he and the other commanders had not noticed, nothing missed the notice of God. He saw it before his angels even conceived the deed in their hearts. This reporting was not for his information, but for his commanders.

All at once, Chamad was escorted before the Throne in chains, escorted between two of Dunastes' top lieutenants, Otsmah and Alaz, whose names meant Triumph. Chamad was a sight to see. He wore the same kind of Earth garment that Dunastes had examined on Makbar, and there was something about his form that was dreadfully altered. His pallor was darkened, and his demeanor was pitiful; and the glory of the Lord had been lifted from him. Perhaps, this was the saddest aspect about him above all.

The arch commanders stood to one side as the great angelic warrior stood in chains with his eyes averted.

"Speak," was the single command from God.

At this, Chamad looked up and about, but avoided the eyes of his top commander, Rhoomai.

"My Lord and my God, I have sinned against you and against heaven. I have nothing to say. Please grant me mercy."

Chamad wept openly before the Throne and before the commanders, and for a moment, Dunastes felt sorry for him. Although this one was not under his command, Chamad was the best of the best. He was mean with a gladius and was held in reputation for the accuracy of his fighting hand. If you placed him in command of a defense maneuver, you knew the job would get done with dispatch. When Cain slew his brother, Abel, and God judged him for the murder, it was Chamad's garrisons who escorted him to the land of Nod for protection.

"Tell me, if you can," replied God, "how you thought to protect the woman by lying with her."

The directness momentarily startled Chamad, and he found himself stuttering like a man. "Satan tempted me with the woman, My Lord, and I did lie with her and espoused her to me as my wife."

The admission brought an audible gasp from the hosts who stood listening, and Rhoomai had to be checked once again by a fierce look from Michael. He had closed his hand around the hilt of his sword again and pulled it several inches from its scabbard. Dunastes saw the move and could relate to it well; he had felt the same way with Makbar.

"Say on," replied God, encouraging Chamad to tell his tale for the benefit of the commanders, whose anger God was relying on.

Many of these that had subverted the laws of heaven would have to be placed in Tartarus until He judged them, and he needed the commanders who would have to imprison them to experience the profound gravity of their crime and to show them no mercy.

"There was a day, My Lord, when I and several battalions of hosts under Yerach's command were commissioned to oversee a remnant of women and children whose men had been slaughtered with the edge of the sword. We had seen this butchery many times before, but this time, the Earth men who were responsible for the massacre went too far." Chamad paused to wipe his face, and his breathing seemed labored and disturbingly human.

"On that day, we fought back many of Satan's emissaries, but this day, he came also among them to fight. We drove back hordes of his devils that surrounded the camp where the women had been taken captive, and our assignment that day was to make sure that none of them were killed. When Satan arrived, it was I who addressed him, and I signaled for my captains to allow him to speak. We were weary, My Lord, from the beatings and the bloodshed, and I wanted to know from Satan what he hoped to achieve. I demanded that he call off his devils and to allow the women to live. This was my assignment, and at this point, I was within my sphere of command."

Rhoomai had settled down, and at this point, he nodded, agreeing with the report as it had been given thus far.

Chamad continued in a halting voice this time. He was about to confess something that was obviously difficult to even speak. "At first, My Lord, I was beside myself with rage, and it was all I could do not to cut him asunder. I do always obey the orders given to me, and not one of my warriors can be accused of sedition, save this one time." At this, he sought out the concurrence of Rhoomai, but then hung his head as he realized the significance of his own words.

In a quiet voice, Chamad continued his accounting. "There was one woman in particular, My Lord, her name is Ashanti who was of interest to me. She is the daughter of the man, Mahalaleel, very fair to look upon, and very gentle. The men of Nod are very violent and greedy men, and they treat their women with contempt and violence. They beat them for the smallest infraction and are most vile in their affections."

At this, Chamad hung his head again, indicating that he had watched.

"None of us intended to give Satan an audience, but I was particularly affected that day when the soldiers took Ashanti intending to rape her. I could take their violence no more, and I wanted to plead her cause with Satan."

Dunastes thought to himself that Chamad had done well thus far, and now, he had ruined it with this last statement. All of them, himself included, had been greatly affected by the violence that was particularly directed against women. He had, himself, on many occasions had to walk away with covered face, knowing that he had no divine license whatsoever to intervene in the atrocities. But to plead with Satan regarding any assigned commission was a whole different matter.

Humph! Dunastes thought to himself, *The day I plead with Satan is the day I plead with him to give me a reason to take my hands from around his neck.*

"My Lord, Satan is clever with his deceit, and he took me in with his words. He mentioned the woman who had become dear to me, and I could see that he had been watching and knew my secret fears about her. He seemed to read my thoughts, and when I tried to make light of my feelings toward her, he knew what to say to trick me. In error, I gave verbal admission to my longing to love and protect her, and before I realized my own undoing, Satan seized the opportunity to examine the real depth of my feelings toward her." Chamad paused again, as the telling of the story seemed to exhaust him.

The commanders who watched him and listened were amazed at his metamorphosing that seemed to take place before their eyes. He had become so human-like in his mannerisms and demeanor that he looked like a fallen angel, who is but one step from falling over the edge.

"Say on," God commanded without pity.

"My mistake with the woman called Ashanti was that when it appeared that they would take her and rape her, I took on the form of a human man, and I murdered the men who intended to assault her. Satan's devils saw me when I did it, and evidently reported the violation to him. I never told her that I was an angel of God; I simply told her that I had come to protect her. My appearance as a human man initially did not calm her as I had hoped; instead, it brought her more fear. My dress and my countenance obviously frightened her, and I had not thought of how your glory upon me would affect her." Chamad hung his head once more, with tears flowing freely. His weakness disturbed the arch commanders, and they found themselves intrigued by the marked decline of this once stalwart warrior.

"Say on," God commanded, wanting the angel to finish so that he could leave His presence forever.

Chamad continued reluctantly; he was about to offer details that would offend the hosts who stood listening. "It hurt me deeply when my appearance brought her confusion and terror. I had meant to calm her and reassure her, but instead, she feared that I was one of those who intended her harm and had come to assault her with stealth. As soon as I left her, Satan came to me and caught me in a moment of disquiet. I still did not see the action that I had taken as wrong, and Satan saw the opening that he needed to lead me further into sin. Had I repented of my error to Commander Rhoomai, he would have set me straight and helped me to see that my feelings toward the woman were an act of sedition." At this, Rhoomai nodded in agreement. Even now, he felt that losing one as fearless as Chamad would result in a deficit to the garrisons under his command.

God nodded for him to continue.

"My hatred for Satan is a pure hatred, My Lord, and the thought that he has won something because of my actions is punishment indeed."

The thought came to God that there was a punishment that awaited Chamad and the others that was so great that nothing could equal it, not even his hatred for Satan.

"You have no idea," was the flat remark from God. "Say on."

"My second mistake, of course, was to give Satan audience, and he questioned me about my longing for the woman. He started with a question, 'Do you not find the woman very fair to look upon, Chamad?' he said to me. 'Has God said that fallen man is to enjoy such a delicate morsel as the woman and not the hosts? God will not know it if you lay with the woman and enjoy her fruit. He does not see everything.'

"My Lord, I did see the trap, but I wanted him to cease and desist in his assaults against the women of the village. I did not want Ashanti to become one of his targets, and had hoped that he, too, saw how special she was above the others."

Dunastes couldn't believe his ears, and it was all he could do to remain silent at such foolishness coming from a superior warrior. His nemesis had gotten away with this right up under the noses of the arch commanders. What a bold strike indeed! Not one of the hosts under the command of these top lieutenants had reported this crime immediately.

"Say on," replied God.

Chamad continued, "I called him a liar and said to him that my will was to do the will of God. I wished that I had left it at that, but he continued to bait me. He then mentioned Ashanti by name and stated to me that he had deliberately not allowed his devils to touch her, as he, too, could see what a treasure she was. Because of my great love for her, Satan's ruse took me in. I was more concerned about perhaps bargaining with him for the protection of her life than any concern of my own. He saw this and took advantage of course."

"He then asked me a question which entrapped me and from which I could not find a detour. He asked me, 'Do you not find the woman, Ashanti, fair, Lieutenant Chamad?' In error, I replied, 'I find her very fair to look upon; she is the most valued among all of the women assigned to me for protection.' Satan immediately capitalized on my error in choice of words. 'Chamad,' he said, 'you have added something to what I said.' At first, I did not catch his ruse, and before I knew it, he led me blindly. 'Of what do you mean, Devil?' I challenged him, and immediately, he reminded me that I added the term 'very' to what he had said about her being fair to look upon." Chamad paused to swallow hard, feeling the weight of his folly.

"I thought that I could compete with the adversary as on equal footing with him, but I was wrong. He caught me in a place where I had refused to be accountable. I felt that because I am a warrior that I was too strong to be led astray of my own desires and longing. The feelings with regard to the woman were so new to me that I confess that there was an intrigue to them that I found intoxicating. I couldn't seem to stop thinking of her and wanting to be with her, and she enchanted my heart with her vulnerability." As the arch commanders listened, they stopped being angry and realized that the story told by Chamad was for their learning, and that what happened to him could surely happen to any one of them if for once they underestimated the sway of one who had once been the Covering Cherub.

Chamad continued without prompting. "Satan then baited me with several statements and even a charge against you, My Lord, which at that moment of my weakness seemed to hold validity. He made sense to me, and it never occurred to me at that moment that he is the father of lies, and there is no truth in him, and whenever he speaks, there is nothing but lies." All of the hosts nodded in unison.

"He said to me, 'I see everything that transpires on the Earth, and I see the way you desire the woman called Ashanti. You wonder what it would be like to fondle and sample something so lovely. Why has God denied the angelic hosts this one sweet indulgence? God is not fair in his dealings with the heavenly host. Have you never stopped to wonder why God would withhold such a prize as the woman from you? He knows that if you and the woman produce fruit of your loins, then you would no longer serve him with your whole heart.'

"My Lord, his words were so compelling, and I did wonder why you have never offered the Woman to us as cohorts." At this, Chamad hung his head in shame, and the other angels were confused that Satan had been so able to deceive him. Dunastes had moved from anger to empathy. At these last words, he was angry again. "Satan must have watched my face; he knew my thoughts and took advantage of my weak longing for the woman's protection. I did wonder about touching the woman in the way that a human man does, and I did wonder what it would be like to copulate with her. I have watched their pleasure of it and wondered about the experience for myself. My Lord, it did not appear to be something that would be painful, but rather pleasurable. I did not see the harm in yielding."

"At this point, the game was over between us, and Satan knew that he had touched the place of my greatest weakness. He led me as a cattle to the slaughter, and as a fool, I placed my head in the stock. Satan continued with me, 'Taste of the Woman's sweet nectar, Chamad,' he said, 'and drink of her honey, for she is comely. Let her breasts satisfy your longing, and her thighs quench your desires! Ever since you first laid eyes on the Woman, you have thought of nothing else!' At this, My Lord, Satan told a lie, but he had taken me, and there was no place of refuge for me. I knew that my desire for the woman was pure, but his logic made sense to me, and his words helped me to face my private longing to enjoy the pleasures of a man with her and to truly protect her so that she would know fear no longer." Chamad began weeping with such power, that many of the hosts, who stood listening, lowered their heads out of respect for him.

"Say on!" God commanded, for Chamad's tears did not move Him at all.

"My Lord, he then brought up the fact that when I appeared to Ashanti as a mortal man, she became afraid of me. His words were not that of rebuke, but counsel, and I found wisdom in what he said." Rhoomai kept swinging in his feelings toward Chamad between pity and exasperation, and this last statement got him stuck in fury.

"He counseled me to appear to her again, but counseled me to reveal my name and to explain to her that I would do anything to win her. He also explained the woman's unique tendencies to me, for oftentimes, I find her perplexing. At times, she appears rather temperamental, and at other times, she seems tender and pliable. Sometimes, her vulnerabilities warm my heart, but then, she will switch up and...."

God gave Chamad a glare that was felt by all. The words stuck in Chamad's throat, and he realized what a blustering fool he must sound like.

"Chamad, do not toy with me today," was all God would say, and nodded for him to continue his tale. He had made the woman and knew exactly what her tendencies were, for He was the One who had put them in her.

Chamad knew to continue this time without the extra commentary. "I did as Satan advised, but did not know that Satan had also dealt with her about me. When I appeared to her the second time, she was completely different toward me. I revealed my secret name to her and won her heart when I spoke of doing anything to win her love and her trust. My Lord, I was smitten, and she captivated me with her ways. I could think of nothing else but the woman, and thoughts of her tortured my mind. I began to neglect my other duties, and I came to a place where I only wanted to be near her to protect her from all harm." Chamad struggled, but knew he must go on and admit all of it no matter how terrible.

"My Lord, she consented to lay with me, and from then on, I knew that my heart belonged to her." Chamad once again hung his head in shame.

Slowly, he lifted his eyes to meet God's direct gaze, but dropped his head again in sorrow. "She is pregnant with my child."

With this last confession, the fallen angel slumped to the floor, while the heavenly hosts gasped in amazement.

Dunastes' mind reeled from the enormity of it all. *Did he say...a child? I didn't know that an angel would even know what to do with a woman, let alone sire a child!*

With the sweep of His hand, God indicated that the tale was finished.

But as an afterthought and before they led Chamad away, God spoke to him with a piercing voice, "By the way, Satan never wins against Me."

As Otsmah and Yerach dragged one of their finest away never to appear before the Throne of God forever, Chamad's hung-down head swayed limply from side to side. It was a sight like none other.

"Put them in chains and confine them to Tartarus immediately!"[37] was the single command made by God. "Prince Michael, you have your orders. Instruct your commanders to collect the others from the Earth, and report back to me immediately when they are under chains of darkness."

Michael nodded and turned swiftly toward the arch commanders, directing them to follow him. The work would be very unpleasant, and none of them looked forward to putting their brothers in chain. It was, without dispute, one of the most difficult things they ever had to do.

When the angels of God mated with the daughters of men, they made the free will choice to forsake their estate as angels and to take on the permanent form of mankind. When they left their habitation and chose the Earth for their abode, the sin and wickedness of

---

[37] Jude 1:6

mankind also corrupted them as well.[38] From their loins, they produced a strange hybrid of angel and man. These became known as mighty men of valor, and they in turn sired children of their own.[39]

The corruption of the bloodline of mankind would produce a deformed race of men that one day mankind would describe, for lack of a better term, as cavemen. But never again in the annals of heaven would God allow such a crime as the mating between his angels and women to occur. From that time forward, man would be commanded and expected to extend his garment over the woman so that she would have power on her head because of the angels. God looked at the sin on the Earth and found it to be so great, that He repented for creating mankind. To clear the slate and to purge man's bloodline, God destroyed the world by water. This was the end of the second Earth.

There was one man left who would carry on the generations of mankind with his family, and that one man's name was Noah.

---

[38] 2 Peter 2:4-5
[39] Genesis 6:4

Chapter 9: Why do the Righteous Suffer?

On the one and only occasion that Satan is known to have told the truth,[40] it involved an incident with a man named Job.

It started out with a routine command that the Sons of God appear before the Throne of God to give an accounting of the works over which they had dominion. Some were principalities and powers whose habitations were in heavenly places, and others had been sent forth to minister to the righteous. Satan was also required to come among them because he won dominion over the works of God's hands in the Earth when Adam sinned. As Dunastes dragged him through the heaven of heavens, the fallen angel was shackled with a gigantic chain that served as handcuffs for his wrists and dropped down the center of his body to encircle his ankles. Although he still had access to heaven, he couldn't just drop in when he felt like it.

When it came to Satan's turn, God opened the dialogue with a question. "Where have you been and what have you been up to?"

God already knew, but in making the demand for accountability, He wanted to rub Satan's nose in it. As the sovereign God, He could take Earth back at any time He felt like it, but He refused to violate the divine laws that He had established from the foundation of the worlds. He had something else in mind that would vindicate mankind and settle the score with Satan forever. Until then, He knew that there were sons of God on the Earth who would, throughout the ages eternally, thwart the plans of Satan. One day, he would have to deal with the man by the name of the Apostle Paul, among a multitude of others, but for now, God decided to give him a taste of Job.

In a surly voice, Satan responded, "I walk to and from and up and down in the Earth to keep an eye on what now belongs to me. The

---

[40] Job 1:10

Man whom you created to be like you is self-centered and is only loyal to you when he requires something of your hand. I find all of them to be one-dimensional—they are quite sensual as beings. There is not one Man on the Earth who will serve you without the promise of gain. The Man is more true to me, than he is to you."

It was all Dunastes could do to keep his composure as his captive spoke. Even when Satan was talking to God, there was a lie in it somewhere.

"Have you considered my servant named Job?"[41] asked God.

The question stunned all who stood there listening. Satan peered at God, momentarily put off by the question that sounded like a challenge. God locked eyes with the deformed being who had once been the most beautiful angel He created and threw down a dare.

"There is no man like Job on the Earth. He is blameless, he walks in righteousness before me, he does not serve me for gain, and he has steadfastly resisted your efforts to entice him."

As the Lord baited Satan, the arch commander Dunastes looked on with interest, wondering what God had in mind to bless the man called Job.

God never jested with Satan, but there was a first time for everything. He kept watching the eyes of the Lord, waiting for him to burst into mocking laughter. When the laughter did not come, Satan stood there running mental calculations, trying to weigh what could play to his best advantage. It was then, upon accepting the Lord's challenge, that the record shows that Satan told the truth about God's unseen hedge of protection around Job.

---

[41] Job 2:3

"Does Job really reverence you because he is true to you? Haven't you built an impenetrable fortress completely surrounding Job, his family, his possessions, and everything he has so that no evil can befall him? I can't get through.[42] You have assigned your angelic champions to build an encampment all about his property and household so that he suffers no loss or mishap. You have enriched him and afforded him manifold and divine favor in everything that he touches, and he is one of the wealthiest men in the Earth. But take the same hand that you have blessed him with, dismiss your warriors from their assignment to guard his life, and destroy everything that is of value to him. You would find out exactly where his loyalties lie, for he would curse you to your face."

As Dunastes looked and listened, the thought came to him that it was a shame that the righteous did not know what Satan knew. If they ever did, they would never fear the liar who stood before him. Dunastes had also taken note of how much mankind wavered in their faith in God's sovereignty. It appeared that any discomfort to their flesh could move them from faith to skepticism, and it didn't appear to take very much to move them.

The Lord already knew what Job would feel, how he would react, and how suffering would intensify something inside of him which would strengthen his resolve until the day of his death.

Not willing that Satan would dictate the terms of the test, however, God moved the challenge into first gear. "Behold, all of his possessions, his family, and his servants, are in your hands to do with as you will, but I forbid you to touch his physical body or that of his wife."

Satan could hardly believe what he was hearing, and neither could the heavenly host. Many of them standing there were charged with the safekeeping and protection of Job and his family and his great

---

[42] Job 1:10

possessions. Some were responsible for taking a hold of the answers to his prayers and delivering them speedily. They could only guess at the degree of suffering which awaited the man they loved so greatly. With the terms of the testing now agreed upon, the Lord withdrew his hedge of protection from Job's family. Satan, on his part, now had the opening he needed, and as the Prince of the Power of the Air, he determined to use every weapon in his arsenal.

Now, this man named Job was the greatest of all men of the East, and he lived in a land known as Uz. He was blameless before God and loved and honored God with his entire household. He was immensely wealthy with seven thousand sheep, three thousand camels, five hundred yoke of oxen, five hundred fertile asses, and a significant household of servants and staff. He also had seven sons and three daughters whom he cherished and prayed for constantly. Although Job did it out of an act of worship and righteousness, every morning, no matter how incredibly wealthy he grew, he covered his household continually by offering up sacrifices and prayers.

He was a man who prayed and fellowshipped with God without ceasing. And, he was no fool. He was a wise man who walked in divine authority, and was fully aware of the protection that his prayers afforded. What he was totally unaware of, however, was that as he prayed continually, he increased the power of his hedge.

One day while his sons and daughters were all gathered for a festive occasion at their eldest brother's house, a messenger came to Job with devastating news. He reported to Job that while his oxen and asses were feeding, a rogue troop of marauders attacked his servants with swords and stole his cattle away. Only he, reported the messenger, was left alive to tell it. But even as the messenger was finishing his last sentence, yet another tragedy hit the man called Job. Another messenger came and reported to him that there had been a sudden volcano eruption that burned up the sheep and consumed the servants in lava, and only he had escaped the destruction to tell it.

Job fell with his face to the ground and grasped his chest in anguish. But before he could take a breath, more destruction came upon him as quickly as Satan could dish it out.

"My lord," came the voice of yet another of his servants, "the Chaldeans came upon the camels in three bands and took them away by force. They have slain your servants who tried to fight to protect them, and only I am left to tell it."

But while this servant was still speaking, yet another came running with tattered and disheveled clothing. "My lord," he began, before the other was finished reporting, "your sons and daughters were eating and drinking in your eldest son's house when a tornado struck the four corners of the house, and it collapsed upon your children. They are all dead, and only I am left to tell it."

At the news of the death of his children, Job tore his mantle, shaved his head, and fell prostrate to the ground in worship to the living God.

Out of the depths, he spoke to his own soul, "Just as I came into this world with nothing, I shall die with nothing. The Lord gave, and the Lord has decided to take it all away. I shall forever look to him who has made the heavens and the earth, and his praises shall continually be on my lips. Blessed be the Name of my God who at all times and in every place has caused me to triumph."

No matter the depths of Job's pain, he refused to sin against God with the words of his mouth. Dunastes looked on at the valiant man made of flesh and was so honored by the man's allegiance that a very interesting proposition came to him. He would, of course, as was the case with the serpent, need God's permission to act on it.

It was on the sad day that Job buried each of his children that Satan once again appeared before God to give an accounting of his activities on the Earth. As was Dunastes' routine, he dragged and harassed the fallen angel all along the way, as they made their journey through the Temple Mount and into the very inner courts of the Almighty God. As the Sons of God gave their accounting, Satan stood peering back and forth at Dunastes. This old champion was a sly one, thought Satan. It was his treachery that caused his armies to be routed by Prince Michael. He could overlook the other angels who had deceived him into thinking that they were for his cause, but he would never forgive Commander Dunastes. How he wished that he could exact vengeance in the courts of heaven just one more time, but Dunastes would beat him to his trick.

When it came Satan's turn, the Lord opened the dialogue. "Where have you been and what have you been up to on the Earth realm?" Satan, who was livid with Job's refusal to yield, really didn't want to talk about it. He had worked overtime, mauling Job's mind with a continuous stream of thoughts that God had allowed the death of his children because of some great sin that he had committed and not repented of. Satan was forbidden to touch the physical body of Job, but was gratified that he could inflict a terrible blow to his faith.

"I've been walking up and down and to and from in the Earth, which belongs to me," Satan replied with an air of contempt.

Dunastes yanked the chain upwards, creating strain on the rivets and causing Satan to bellow with rage.

"You dare to address Yahweh with insolence?" growled Dunastes.

He entertained the thought of taking the loose end of the chain and tightening it around Satan's neck until his one remaining head burst open, but knew that he would just grow another one right back in its place. The Lord heard the thoughts of his top commander and checked Dunastes with a look of displeasure. He knew that Dunastes hated this assignment of escorting Satan through the heaven of heavens, but He also knew that Satan hated it much more.

When the moment passed, Satan continued slyly but in a much-reserved tone, "The Man whom you have created in your image and has your likeness is shallow and faithless. He is only interested in trinkets and baubles and can be bought of the highest bidder. You have made a mistake in creating mankind. They are of no consequence to me."

"Have you considered my servant Job?" asked God.

Satan was stunned to silence. He locked eyes with God only half believing what he was hearing. For a moment, he distrusted God, knowing that there was something at stake that would probably fall out to God's best interests. But because his nature was so corrupted and degraded, the thought of inflicting further evil on the man who had steadfastly refused to curse God was too intoxicating to ignore. He looked to Dunastes who seemed unmoved, then back to God who was anticipating his acceptance of the next phase of the challenge.

The Lord continued, "There is no man like Job on the Earth. He is blameless, he walks in righteousness before me, he does not serve me for gain, and he steadfastly refuses your enticements. Although you have convinced me to remove the hedge that protects him from all of your assaults, still, he maintains his integrity before me. Although his sorrow and pain is great, he would rather die than renounce me."

Satan was quick with his retort, "Is that true, my Lord? Yea, skin for skin is the real contest. I am very acquainted with what is of most value to this man. Although his children are dead and his possessions are lost, they are easily replaceable. But take the same hand which has blessed and protected him, and touch him with disease and sickness, and he will, without fail, curse you to your face."

It was time to move the contest to the final phase, but to make sure that Satan would not dictate the terms, God replied, "Yes, I will remove the hedge and allow you to take his health, but you are forbidden to cause his death as a result of your attacks."

At this, Satan laughed with unbridled joy. The Lord checked Dunastes with another glance. It came just as the commander was about to pull his sword from its scabbard.

So, Satan went forth from the presence of the Lord and wasted no time in torturing Job's body. Since he was forbidden to put a disease on him that would waste him and cause his death, he struck Job with loathsome, puss-filled boils that covered him from the soles of his feet to his face. They burned with fire as they spread to every inch of the skin on his body. His pain and suffering was incredible. No matter how he tried to sit or lay, the open, fetid tumors drew worms that sickened him to his stomach. As each tumor healed over, it developed a repulsive, itching scab. Job sat down in a heap of smoldering ashes, finding that this prevented the growth of the worms, and scraped his scabs with a potsherd. It was in the ashes that his wife found him half naked and half crazed with private suffering.

His wife now challenged him with the same words used by Satan. "Do you still believe in the justice of God?"[43] she spat at her husband. "Curse Him to His face and give up the ghost so that your suffering will end as well as mine! Whatever sin you have committed which has brought this great destruction to our lives is too much for me to bear."

As the angelic host stood watching and protecting Job from death, they were stunned by his reply to his wife.

Slowly, and with agonized breathing, he said to her, "You talk like the foolish women of the city talk. Is this the voice of my wife? What? Are we to love God when He is good to us, and not when He turns His face from us? Are we to receive blessings of His hands, but not evil as well? Blessed be the Name of the Lord forever; I commit my spirit into His hands!" With that, the man called Job bowed his head in misery and shame.

---

[43] Job 2:9,10

Job's wife stooped to gather dirt and ashes in her hands and tossed them into the face of her husband as a last dishonorable assault to his manhood.

Although Job had faced the worst of his losses, there was still yet one more insult that he must endure. And it would be at the hands of the people he called his friends. It happened over several days, but began on a morning when he least expected any company at all. His name had become synonymous with disgrace in the entire land of Uz, and the same people whom he had once helped and counseled, now shunned him, believing him to be cursed by God.

At first, it was just three of them to be joined by a fourth, but when they saw him from afar, they did not recognize him from the toll that the disease and emotional stress had caused. He resembled a walking skeleton, and the loose skin of his face sagged in folds about his neck. Sores covered his entire body, and he stank from the running puss and blood. He was black from the soot of the ashes, and the streaks from his unending tears ran from the lids of his eyes to his mouth. The prolonged suffering changed him into a different man, but in all this, he did not sin against God with his mouth.

On the day that Eliphaz, Bildad, Zophar,[44] and later, Elihu saw Job as he sat in his ashes, they lifted their voices and wept the weeping of men. They each tore his mantel and threw dust upon their heads toward the heavens. When they saw how great his grief was, they sat on the ground for seven full days with him, and out of respect, spoke not a word. It was when they opened their mouths and presumed to speak for God, that their words got them into trouble with God. In the end, God would not turn the captivity of Job until he forgave Eliphaz, Bildad, and Zophar for their stout charges against him. Each of them voiced their opinion in lengthy soliloquies, that the destruction of Job's health, wealth, and family had come at the hand of God, and they

---

[44] Job 2:11-13

each believed that Job had brought it on himself through sin. They were wrong on many different levels.

The Lord blessed Job double for his trouble.[45] As his friends, acquaintances, and brothers and sisters came to visit him to pity him for his distresses; they each brought a piece of money with them and jewelry made of the purest gold. So, the Lord blessed the end of the man Job more than at the beginning, for God blessed him with fourteen thousand sheep, six thousand camels, a thousand yoke of oxen, and a thousand fertile female asses. God also blessed Job with long life and restored his youth and vigor. He was blessed with the birth of seven more sons and three daughters who were reputed to be the most beautiful women in the whole of the land. After this, Job lived for one hundred and forty more years of life and witnessed the birth of four generations of his children's children. Then, he died, being of great age and full of life. But there was one last footnote in Job's story that involved the champion, Dunastes.

There was a man by the name of Moses whom God would speak to face to face. God loved this man and entrusted him with the deliverance of His chosen people. Moses was not just God's man and leader, but under the inspiration of God's Spirit, would go on to write many books of what man would come to call the Bible.

One night during his life, Dunastes visited this man called Moses. On permission from God, Dunastes dragged Satan in shackles to the bedside of the man called Moses as a witness to the proceedings. While in a night vision which would haunt him for days, Moses saw the form of an imposing angelic champion. He stood thirteen feet in stature, with eyes that pierced like a lance. His ornately decorated mantle was the color of crimson, denoting an officer of considerable rank. The emerald, carbuncle, and chrysoprasus garnished the crest of his breastplate, and the color of his shin greaves were gold emboldened with purple. In the vision of his bed, Moses saw what

---

[45] Job 42:9-17

appeared to be a sheathed gladius at the side of the commander, and fixed to his girdle was a pugio.

It was then that he saw Satan in his fallen form, standing beside the mighty angel in chains and shackles. As Moses looked on in the visions of his bed, he saw and heard a wonder from heaven. There was a conversation that took place in heaven between Satan and God, involving a servant of God named Job. This man was tested beyond the endurance of any normal man, and although he lost everything, he still had God.

As Moses watched and listened, Dunastes touched his mind to imprint the dialogue in his memory. Satan stood watching, almost beside himself with rage. One of his most effective weapons against mankind was the question of his existence. With this revelation given to the man called Moses, his testing of the man called Job would now go into the eternal record for all of mankind to examine and interpret.

In his waking hours, the night vision seemed to pursue the man called Moses. As the vision hounded him, Moses sat down finally and penned these words, "There was a man in the land of Uz, whose name was Job; and that man was perfect and upright, and one who feared God, and eschewed evil...."

Never again, in the annals of the sacred record, would such an extraordinary revelation as this conversation occur between Satan and God in heaven. On his part, Dunastes added another notch to his pugio.

Chapter 10: Twenty-One Days

There was war in heaven. Satan issued an all-points directive for ten thousand times ten thousands of his garrisons to prepare an ambushment against the Archangel Gabriel, but he underestimated the power of a prophet's prayer. In fact, its impact was how the devils knew that Gabriel was on the move.[46]

As the man, Daniel, fasted and prayed, his prayers caused a major upheaval in the heavens that had an immediate impact. Satan's kingdom was divided into principalities first, and then powers, rulers of darkness, and spiritual wickedness in high places. Of these, a principality named Yarat, whose name means Perverse, ruled as king over the land of Persia. He was an ancient foe. Tens of thousands of Yarat's mounted cavalry met in response to the terror caused by Daniel's intercession. Not only had Daniel's prayers reached heaven, but they also turned Yarat's kingdom upside down. Devils were sent from every corner of the heavens, and only the fittest and most gallant were recruited to participate in the massive operation. There was but one command issued from Satan himself, and that command was that Gabriel must be stopped.

Yarat set his top lieutenants on the western front and dispatched his mounted cavalry into position on the east. Gabriel had been first sighted over the Persian Gulf, making his descent over the Caspian Sea. If he could catch the gigantic archangel unawares, he would take him captive and realize a remarkable coup. As his most able demons of darkness came quickly in response to his summons, he strategized and planned for every possible contingency. The Archangel Gabriel must be stopped! With a voice that screamed like a windstorm and red eyes that burned with malice, he made it clear to all that they were not to bother to return if they failed to come back without Gabriel in chains.

---

[46] Daniel 9:20-23

On the day the military operation was scheduled to go down against Gabriel, something went dreadfully awry. Satan was in an uproar, and his closest lieutenants were at a loss for words. Daniel's prayers were shattering major strongholds and pummeling some of Satan's most resilient regimes and powers. Other than the man, Jeremiah, Yarat could hardly remember any one man's prayers causing such devastation. They knew that they had to stop Gabriel from getting to him, but they also had to stop Daniel.

To meet the offensive on both objectives, Satan sent his armies to thwart the man, Daniel, and to kill him if possible, unaware that God's angels were already in position and waiting for his first strike. Had he known Dunastes was the commander in charge of the garrisons to protect Daniel, he would not have even bothered. Just as special forces of Yarat's devils moved in stealth against Daniel at the great river Hiddekel, Dunastes' warriors seemed to descend from out of nowhere. As the angels of God fought the angels of Satan, the battle went back and forth for several days. On the third day of the fighting, Dunastes' garrisons finally drove Yarat's infantry into retreat. He left them there with Otsmah in charge and readied his gladius for the next fight.

While Dunastes had been protecting Daniel, several of God's arch commanders were with Gabriel when Yarat's offensive against him was initiated as he moved from the third heaven into the second heavens of the land of Persia. Gabriel had gotten no further than a kilometer when Yarat's forces met him swinging double-edged swords with dangerous accuracy. This peculiar division of devils never missed. Rhoomai and Chrioni's garrisons threw an innumerable company of elite warriors against Yarat's divisions, and the battle waged on...for twenty-one days. These devils had only one objective in mind: the Archangel Gabriel must be stopped.

On the twenty-second day of the battle, several more of Yarat's reserve garrisons advanced against God's most valiant warriors. This time, they momentarily pushed back Rhoomai's forces, leaving Chrioni's lieutenants in a vulnerable position and forcing the arch commander to rely on his most tenuous garrisons. Steel against steel cut the curtains of the second heavens in tatters, and for a time, the men on the Earth thought the world was about to end. It was when Gabriel looked up almost too late to see Yarat come at him with his sword in full swing, that Prince Michael swung first and with one blistering strike sent Yarat plummeting to the Earth. Rhoomai's forces quickly recovered, while two more arch commanders buttressed Chrioni's front lines.

The hordes of beaten devils fled into the darkness to nourish their wounds, but Prince Michael knew that they were by no means defeated. He ordered Dunastes' forces to remain with the man, Daniel, and discharged Rhoomai's forces to provide clear escort for Gabriel through the second and first heavens. He knew that Dunastes would handle it from there.

When Gabriel got there, Daniel was in fervent prayer. Something of an unusual energy and authority quickened him and even caused him to tremble. Once, when he looked up from prayer because he felt something touch him, he was stunned to see the messenger of God named Gabriel. Though he had the appearance of a man, he stood more than nine feet in stature, and it was obvious to Daniel that he was no ordinary man. He was clothed in white linen, with a girdle about his loins encrusted with the fine gold that originated from Uphaz. His magnificent body had the appearance of beryl, and his eyes were as lamps of fire. His arms and feet were the color of polished brass, and the sound of his voice was the voice of a multitude.[47]

When Gabriel first appeared to him, Daniel saw him as one in a vision, and for fear of the archangel, every ounce of Daniel's strength left him. As he fell to his face, the sight of the great angel struck terror in his soul. He had never seen an angelic being of such majesty and beauty. The presence of one as mighty as Gabriel put Daniel in a deep sleep for two hours. From somewhere afar off, he heard the voice of the angel, but his muscles seemed disengaged, and he could not move

---

[47] Daniel 10:2-12

his head or his torso. A hand touched him and strengthened him, and it was then that he noticed that the men who had been with him in prayer and fasting had all fled away. They never saw what Daniel saw, but the sound of Gabriel's voice caused as much terror as the sight of him had caused to Daniel.

The weighty hand that touched him seemed to lift him with authority and tremendous strength. It placed him upright on his knees, but then, Daniel faltered again and found himself buckling once again under the heaviness of the anointing. The hand of the one named Gabriel touched him again, and Daniel was able to steady his weight by shifting most of it to the palms of his hands. When he was finally able to come up to a kneeling position, his vision cleared, and he was able to peer up and into the eyes of the Messenger of God.

"O, Daniel, a man greatly beloved of God," was the way the Archangel addressed the man. "I need you to not fear me, but stand upright on your feet and hearken to what I have to say to you. I am sent specifically to talk to you."

As Daniel struggled to stand to his feet, his emotions and thoughts were a jumble of confusion, and his knees wanted to buckle again. He felt his blood begin to drain in the right direction, but he had tremors in his hands and mouth, and he found it hard to breathe. He tried to focus on something else other than the angel's eyes, and this seemed to help. The very glory that radiated from the aura of the angel was like looking into the very face of God. There was no doubt that this angel stood often in God's presence, and at His very throne.

Daniel's whole body trembled as the great being continued to speak for he had never been in the presence of such anointing in all of his life, "Daniel, don't be afraid," the angel spoke with firmness but also with a consideration for his humanity. "From the very first day that you set your heart to understand what God has purposed for you and your people, and you decided to deny your appetites so that you

When Kingdoms Fall

could hear from heaven, your words were heard at that very moment, and I have now come in response to your prayers."

Daniel could hardly believe his ears, and he felt like he was about to faint again. He tried not to look into the eyes of the angel, but they seemed to draw him in like tongues of fire. He looked quickly away again to balance his weight, but his legs felt like no strength remained in them at all. And though he had eaten no food for three weeks and more, there were times when he felt bile come up from his stomach to his mouth. His whole insides burned, and he was drenched in his own body fluids. For a moment, he doubted if he would be able to stand in the angel's presence to hear more.

Gabriel saw the man's weakness and tried to continue. "Because I have come to give understanding to the visions you have had concerning the future state of your people, I want you to know what delayed my coming. When I was sent to you, there was a mighty demon of darkness of the kingdom of Satan known as the Prince of Persia who withstood me for twenty-one days in a fight.[48] But as I fought with him to get to you, Prince Michael, one of the archangels of the Lord, came to help me fight, and he and I fought side by side with the demons who control the kings of Persia." Gabriel paused to gain a sense of where the man was, and was relieved to see that he was doing a little better. Although he still stood trembling on his feet, he was a mess. He was crying, he was wet with perspiration, there were tremors that shook his body from head to foot, and he still had not tried to speak.

Gabriel tried to continue, "I have now come to make you understand what is to become of your people in the final days of this age, for the visions you have seen are yet many generations away. You have seen far." Just as Gabriel had spoken the last phrase, Daniel fell once again on his face to the ground. That was when Dunastes intervened.

---

[48] Daniel 10:13-15

He had actually been standing there all along, but the man, Daniel, was in such a state from the appearance of the Archangel Gabriel, that he was afraid that if he saw both of them together, it would be too much on his heart and cause his physical death. When Daniel fainted again, this time, Gabriel retreated a safe distance to give Dunastes the opportunity to minister to him. The clarity of the man's ability to see into the spirit realm was of unusual strength and accuracy. Normally, when Gabriel appeared to mankind, they saw through a glass darkly and did not see so much as to cause the injury as it now did to Daniel. It spoke much of the man's consecration.

Dunastes knelt to touch the man, Daniel, and set him in a seated position. As the man trained his vision, he was able to look at Dunastes without wavering. They sat for quite a while as Dunastes kept his hands on the man's shoulders to impart strength into his muscles and to regulate the circulation of his blood again. It worked. Dunastes imparted supernatural strength to the tissues and organs that had been deprived of oxygen, minerals, and water as a result of the fasting. He needed the man strong and coherent for the message that Gabriel must give to him. When his eyes cleared and Daniel reached up to touch Dunastes on his arm, they both knew the danger of losing the man was nearly over.

Dunastes then touched his lips, and Daniel looked up and now saw both of them without faltering. "O, my Lord!" he cried looking toward Gabriel, "because of my visions, sorrow and pains have gotten the best of me physically, and I can't seem to regain enough strength to even hear what you have to say. How can I talk to the very Messenger of God, when I am so weak and feeble?[49] The glory which is upon you is too much for me, and I am unable to stand up under it, being but a human man." Daniel was gulping for air and trying desperately to regain himself. Dunastes touched him once again, and this final touch regulated his electrolytes.

---

[49] Daniel 10:16-19

Gabriel walked slowly to where Daniel was, towering above him, and then thought better of trying to have the man stand. He nodded for Dunastes to stay seated with him and was thankful that the man was now strengthened enough to converse with him. If Daniel was able to speak, then it was an excellent sign that he could hear as well.

"O man greatly beloved of God!" Gabriel tried again, "do not be afraid of me. Peace be unto you, Servant of God! Be strong, Yea, be strong, and do not be afraid."

This time, Gabriel's very words strengthened Daniel, and he responded with clarity, "Let my lord say on, for you have strengthened me."[50]

Dunastes stayed with him to keep an eye on him, for it was his assignment to make sure that the man was protected from harm as well as danger.

Grateful now that Daniel was out of danger, Gabriel began to share with Daniel the meaning of his night visions concerning Israel. As he spoke, Daniel was astounded by the revelation imparted to him. The interpretation of the visions had plagued him to the point of prayer. As Gabriel clarified the symbols in his visions, he also gave him great understanding in the writings which had been passed to him by the patriarchs of old. When he was done, Gabriel and Michael stood to leave him, both anxious to get back to assist Prince Michael. Daniel watched them go in startled wonder, and for many days after could not believe that what he experienced had not been just mere visions.

When Gabriel and Dunastes cleared the first heaven, the second heavens were thick with demons over Persia and Greece. Garrisons of God's best fighters were already engaged when the two commanders arrived, and Dunastes was pleased to see that Prince Michael was holding his own without them.

---

[50] Daniel 10:17-21

Just as Dunastes reached to grab his pugio, with a grin, Gabriel grabbed his wrist. "My friend, it is always a pleasure to fight side by side with you, but the first strike belongs to me."

Dunastes laughed and threw his pugio to Gabriel and yanked his gladius from its scabbard with a cry of triumph. They joined Michael at the moment that he routed thousands of Satan's best champions, with one foot on the star, Alula Borealis, and one hand behind his back.

Section Two

The Scepter from Judah

Chapter 11: When Kingdoms Fall

The Son of God had lived in obscurity almost all of his human life. Although he was the God-Man, meaning he was very God and very Man, he had never made a claim to deity; he did no miracles, walked wherever he had to go, ate and slept like other normal men, laughed when he found something funny, and wept when he found something sad. If it had not been for his extraordinary birth, which caused a great deal of commotion in the spirit realm, the fact of his existence could have easily passed without even a footnote to the historical record.

At the age of twelve,[51] he was seen debating in the Temple with the scribes and elders, but then, he disappeared into the drudgery of human life, and Satan became convinced that the whole thing had been a ruse. There were many before him who had appeared on the Earth scene and made the claim of being the long-awaited Messiah of the Jews. Once they were found to be nothing more than mortal men, Satan was convinced that God's judgment of him in the Garden had been nothing more than words. Still, he had his devils keep an eye on Jesus as a matter of course. If indeed he were a king, he was not much to look at, and there was nothing about him that one would find captivating. Soon, Jesus would think the same about Satan, but with a more valid frame of reference.

Everything on the Earth realm was going steadily and in accordance with Satan's plans, until the day that Dunastes showed up at his door. The great angelic commander appeared with several of his lieutenants at his side and brazenly demanded respect of Satan's devils on his own turf.

"How dare you enter my domain without invitation, Commander!" Satan shouted at him. "Why have you come, and whom do you seek?"

---

[51] Luke 2:42-52

115

Having one of God's most elite warriors sent to him with a matter to discuss, was extremely threatening to Satan. The glory of God enveloped each of the angelic champions and was a stark reminder of what he used to be and what he used to have. He didn't like entertaining these kinds of thoughts and was impatient for Dunastes to state his business and to take his leave.

"I have come," stated Dunastes with great effect, "to call you to a battle."

The demonic champions around Satan reacted immediately by pulling their swords. Dunastes just looked at them and sneered. There was one among them that he recognized as one of the most gallant warriors in heaven before his fall, but these others did not warrant distress even on his worse day. He glanced at the captains who had accompanied him and indicated to them that they were to remain unruffled.

"Instruct your devils to stand down before I hurt one of them by mistake," was the flat order from the arch commander who was as serious with the threat as he could be.

Satan turned slowly and nodded for them to sheath their weapons, but then several of them stepped up close to him as if to shield him from Dunastes. The move angered Dunastes, and it was all he could do to keep his composure. So far, he was doing just fine with what God had told him to do, but he knew that if Satan's devils kept up their antics, he would have cause to repent.

Satan faced him squarely but was greatly unnerved by his bold statement. He decided to bluff him to aggravate him just a little, "You are foolish to come alone, Commander Dunastes. Where are your garrisons? Have you come to do battle with me alone?" Satan spoke slowly and deliberately, and kept watching Dunastes with suspicion as if he were expecting angelic soldiers to jump from behind the nearest bushes. He hated all of God's arch commanders with a special hatred, but this one that stood before him was the bane of his existence.

"It is not with me, Devil, that you are being summoned to battle. It is with the Son of God. You are being given permission to test him in order to prove him, but you are forbidden to lay a hand on him." Dunastes stated the information without emotion and as if he were giving it to an underling.

Satan peered at him, incredulous. He had long since come to doubt the words of the human prophets that Jesus would one day come in human flesh.

Dunastes continued, "You may test him, and you may transport him, but nothing more. You will come with me now, and I will take you to where he is. Your devils are forbidden to accompany you." Dunastes stated it all with a quiet authority and made it clear from his manner that there was no negotiation of terms permitted.

Satan was suspicious and wondered if it was all another trap. "You say that there is one who walks the Earth and who claims to be the Son of God?"

Satan did not try to hide his surprise. Satan turned and looked at the devils that stood with him, and they all laughed, but it was nervous laughter. "How is he known among men, and where is his abode?"

At this point, Satan moved closer to Dunastes, and the gigantic angel closed his hand around the hilt of his gladius. He was standing there with his lieutenants who were greatly outnumbered by Satan's devils.

"He is known as Jesus, the son of Joseph and Mary, of the root of King David and of the tribe of Judah. He was born in the city of David in a town called Bethlehem, and he is a Nazarene by citizenship and a carpenter by trade." The commander watched the face of the Devil as he gave information that had been well guarded from the bastions of darkness.

"He has walked among men in a body of human flesh for thirty years, and this is now the hour of his appointed time. Your kingdom must come down."

The news now brought a chatter of disbelief throughout the ranks of the devils.

Satan appeared unmoved by the declaration, but inwardly, there was great turmoil. As a bluff, he retorted, "Can any good thing come out of Nazareth?"

"Very well, Commander Dunastes," hissed Satan to cover his agitation, "by all means take me to the 'Savior' of the world. Your prophets have spoken so highly of him, and I am most anxious to finally have an audience with him," mocked Satan.

Dunastes turned and locked eyes with his ancient foe and added for his ears only, "No weapon that you fashion against him will work. And no matter what happens, one day, you and I will stand face to face alone and settle our score forever!" growled the archangel to the devil.

Not wanting him to have the last say, Satan retorted, "You think more highly of yourself than you ought, Commander. I was there on the day you were created. You are nothing more than feathers and wings. You will always be my inferior! When I am finished with your 'Savior,' I am coming for you next, Arch Commander Dunastes!" he spat.

On cue, thousands of devils pressed forward to flank Satan, and the hardest thing Dunastes ever had to do was capitulate.

This particular battle would take place in a wilderness, just miles from the legendary banks of the Jordan River. In preparation, Jesus had been led here of the Holy Spirit for many days and nights alone. Although the angels of God had been commissioned to watch the proceedings, they were forbidden to intervene or minister to him until the victory was won. What would happen here in a matter of days would not just overturn Satan's right to rule the Earth, but it would lay the Chief Cornerstone for what would become known as the Church.

As the small group sped quickly past the pillars of the Earth, they came to a region in Galilee that was familiar to Satan, but not often visited. Demons hated dry, desolate places. When they got there, Dunastes reluctantly backed off a great distance, and Satan was momentarily stunned to see that indeed, the God-Man appeared defenseless and alone. He could see the angelic champions nearby— they were the fittest of God's commanders. Could this indeed be the one whom the prophets spoke so highly of?

When they arrived, Jesus had been fasting for more than thirty days and nights.[52] Although he saw Satan's arrival, he did not respond. The battle would not begin until his fortieth night was finished. In the meantime, Satan watched him from a distance. He studied him closely as a hunter would stalk its quarry and noted that the God-Man had taken no food. The fasting had weakened him physically. Still, he dared not underestimate the strength of this, his greatest enemy.

On the forty-first day, Satan's approach signaled the start of the fight, and he was not about to yield the ground even for formalities. He was an ancient foe and knew the constitution of the human body about as well as the One who created it. He decided to test the strength of the ego first, through the appetite of the flesh.

"Prove that you are the Son of God," bellowed Satan. "If you are whom you claim to be, demonstrate your power by commanding these rocks to be turned into bread!"

---

[52] Matthew 4:1-3

Jesus was so weak from the fasting and the exposure to the elements, that he felt lightheaded and even dizzy as he moved slowly to Satan's right. The move bothered Satan, and he moved counter to him as a sign of resistance. Jesus had never once used his supernatural power as a human man, and the slow movement to Satan's right was calculated intentionally to distract. At the thought of using his divine power to satisfy a longing of his flesh, the God-Man was at once repulsed and privately observed that it was a poor choice for a first temptation.

He then ignored the rocks completely. He had spent forty days sleeping on them, sitting on them, looking at them, and praying on them. Turning them into something to eat was the last thing he would have done to satisfy his hunger.

In a calm voice, Jesus responded to the fallen angel, "It is written; Man cannot live by bread alone, but by every word that proceeds out of the mouth of God."

The finality and authority with which the God-Man spoke startled Satan. Momentarily, he was caught off guard and tried to mentally regroup himself. The God-Man had just won the first strike without breaking a sweat. From henceforth and forevermore, Man had just been granted the power to deny his own flesh.

Satan took a moment to size up his prey. Perhaps, he had underestimated the fortitude of his contender, but he did not believe for one moment that the one who stood before him was God, the Son, in the bodily form of flesh.

"You are to come with me," was all that Satan would say to move the next temptation into play.

They traveled faster than the speed of sound to the city of Jerusalem, and there, Satan directed the Son to sit on the highest apex of the Temple.

"Prove that you are the Son of God!" Satan bellowed in the face of Jesus. "If you are who you claim to be, cast yourself down from here, for it is also written, He shall give his angels charge concerning thee: and in their hands, they shall bear thee up, lest at any time thou dash thy foot against a stone."[53]

Momentarily, the dizzying height took its toll on Jesus. His head was swimming from the lack of food, and he found it difficult to maintain control over the dark thoughts that bullied his mind. There were times when dark shadows crossed in front of his line of vision, and he wondered if he was beginning to hallucinate. He found himself clutching the tip of the massive apex, and the thought came to him that he would surely fall.

"Prove who you say you are! If you are whom you claim to be, you will never hit the ground!" Satan spat at him.

Jesus began to feel tremors in his legs and hands, and his heart fluttered uncontrollably. At times, it felt easier to just let go into a free fall from his perch on the Temple. He looked up at the garrisons of angels stationed a good distance before him and felt a quiet reassurance that they would not allow him to hit the ground. If he just let go, they would catch him, and perhaps, this part of the fight would be over. He felt the desperate need to lay his head down if for just one moment, but there was nowhere to lay his head. When he realized how dangerous the train of thought was, he realized that Satan was fighting him on more than one level.

The height had caused his mouth to dry out, but the God-Man swallowed hard and steeled himself against the assault. He then locked eyes with his opponent and replied in a firm, steady voice, "It is written again, Thou shalt not tempt the Lord thy God."

---

[53] Matthew 4:6-11

Though brief, there was such a tremendous authority to what he said that Satan felt the words hit him like a jackhammer. It stunned him, and he stared at Jesus, not wanting to believe that he had just lost the second strike. From henceforth and forevermore, Man had just been granted the supernatural authority of the Mind of Christ over every form of mental distress and abuse.

Dunastes and the angelic hosts couldn't believe the brazen test that had just taken place in the holy place and in the Holy City. If in fact Jesus had bowed to the challenge, they would have no other choice but to catch him before he struck the Temple grounds. That Jesus had just routed the fallen angel in the greatly weakened physical state that he was in, caused the valiant, tough commander to admire him the more. The commander longed to impart strength with a touch, but he knew that this was forbidden. His very heart ached for the Son of God. He would greatly rejoice when this test of obedience was over, for he had been told of the great suffering that still lie ahead of him at the hands of mortal men.

For the final strike, the Devil took the Son of God up into an exceedingly high mountain and used his powers to give Jesus a panoramic view of all of the kingdoms of the world at once. The visual assault of colors, textures, splendor and majesty was intoxicating and almost drove Jesus to his knees. He saw grandeur on a magnificent scale and camels laden with ivory and jewels. He saw the allure of diamonds and raw gold, and the finery of silk and pearls. He saw great pillars of marble and the finest tapestry and cedar. He felt that he was in the center of a great vortex, with his head spinning out of control.

The Devil watched him closely and kept changing the vista as he saw the God-Man begin to wither under the attack. All doubt was now gone. He knew that the One who stood before him was none other than the very Son of God. They had once walked as brothers in the heaven of heavens, and now, here he was in human flesh. It was unbelievable that the Earth prophets had been right about him coming to the Earth in a baby form and growing into manhood.

"All of these things I will give you right now if you will fall down and worship me!" Satan seemed beside himself with excitement.

What a coup it would be to get Jesus to throw his allegiance. By Satan's estimation, Jesus had given up his abode in the heaven of heavens and had become a human man to build a kingdom on the Earth for his Father. But if he could convince Jesus that he could have his own kingdoms apart from his Father's whims, they would each win what they wanted the most…he thought. It never occurred to Satan that the very purpose of the coming of Jesus in the flesh was to do the will of his Father.[54]

It took a few moments to stop his head from spinning, but when it did, Jesus responded with such a voice of conviction that it shook the heavens, "Get behind me, Satan! For it is written, 'Thou shalt worship the Lord thy God, and Him only shalt thou serve!'"

The dark angel threw his head back and roared as much in disappointment as in the agony of defeat. From henceforth and forevermore, Man would have the conquering power to decide what he would give his worship to. Satan turned quickly to leave Jesus, but then briefly turned back to peer at him.

His parting words, just before Dunastes drew his sword, were, "You have won nothing. I still own the Earth, and you cannot take what rightfully belongs to me! We shall meet again, soon, and this time, it will be on my terms!" With that, Satan departed quickly, and with his departure, the angels of God came to minister to Jesus and to see him safely back to his dwelling.

In a twist of divine irony, Satan didn't know that when Jesus looked at the splendor of each earthly kingdom, with the eyes of God, he also saw their fall.

---

[54] 1 Timothy 3:16

Chapter 12: A Memorial to the Woman

On the morning that the woman set out for Simon the leper's house,[55] she passed through the village of Bethphage near the eastern slope of the Mount of Olives to get there. It was a short distance, but as she walked, her female emotions dragged her in several different directions. The roads were not good, but as she traveled, she passed many other travelers going in the same direction.

She had been up all night, weighted down with the burden of something that felt big and even risky. She couldn't fight the feeling that her life depended on what she was about to do. She was afraid and excited all at the same time and wondered if it showed on her face. The assignment that drove her left little room for small talk, and she deliberately avoided the streets that she knew would force her to walk past the homes of her sister-girls. She loved them, God knows, but she refused to be sidetracked today by idle gossip and gainsaying.

She had just made it past a critical bend in the road when she heard somebody's voice call out her name. She turned just quickly enough to wave a friendly hello, but refused to discover the identity of the acquaintance. She was too afraid that if she stopped even for a moment, that the bigness of what she was about to do would give her cause to rethink her mission. She must do this, no matter what, even though she knew that it might be the final blow to her reputation.

As she kept walking, she tucked her head under the mantle that had been given to her by Jesus and speeded up her pace as she noticed that the morning traffic was getting heavier. The merchants were out and about, unloading their camels and hawking their goods in the streets. Many of them stopped momentarily to peer at the lone, female figure and recognized who she was without comment. When this day was over, those who already disdained her would finally have cause to

---

[55] Matthew 26:6-13

fully hate her. Many things played in her memory, but chief among them was the day that she first met Jesus. She marveled at the juxtaposition of her life with his, and how her meeting him that day in the temple had changed her life forever.

At the time that the incident which rocked Bethany occurred, she was a married woman involved in an adulterous affair with this man who was himself married. The good wine had long since run out in her marriage. She foolishly languished in a meaningless relationship with a man who was not her husband, but who had promised her the sky without a moon anywhere in it. There were many in the city who were out to get her, but even to that day, she suspected that it was probably her lover's wife who was behind the breaking of the scandal. She was only partly right—the unseen mastermind behind the plot was actually Satan himself. There was a much bigger fish to hook than just the woman, for it was Jesus whom Satan wanted most of all. But as God would have it, it was time for a woman to finally teach Satan a lesson that he would not soon forget.

Early one morning, as she languished too long in her lover's arms, she heard the loud noise of the door to her home being broken open. She tried to jump up to cover her nakedness, but her lover held her in a vise with his eyes locked on hers. Even as she thought back on the incident that occurred that infamous morning, her heart still could not believe that he would betray her in his arms. But of such is the fabric of setups. Before she could even cry out, the drapes to her private bedchamber were ripped down, and she looked up into the foul eyes of more than a dozen Pharisees and elders. Her two-timing lover finally released her eyes and climbed out of her bed, leaving her to face her assailants alone.

She was stunned as she watched him snatch up his garments, never looking back once with even a glance of pity. The mob that stood before her parted their ways to allow him to leave, and it was as clear as day to her then what a fool she'd been. Three of the temple magistrates laid their vile hands upon her nude body and fondled her as they made sport of her predicament. Two of them slapped her about and shamed her with their eyes. All of them made merriment as they tried to strip her of any vestige of her female dignity that she had left. Not far from where she stood, Dunastes watched as well, but he was emotionless. Because of her pre-ordained connection to Jesus, he was on special assignment to make sure that this woman was avenged of the great evil done to her this day. And what a mighty avenging that would be!

As they dragged her through the streets of Bethany with fake pomp and melodrama, many of her neighbors went out of their way to spit at her. The women of the city covered their faces in shame of her, and the men spat obscenities and mocked her as she was jerked along. She limped, barefoot and bruised, as they dragged her by her hair. All the while, she kept trying to pull her clothing about her body to hide her nakedness.

Many yelled from windows, "Away with her! Stone her! She has violated Moses's law!" Others yelled, "Adulteress, away with you adulteress! Stone her. Stone the adulteress!"

In a haze, she kept wondering where they were taking her because instead of taking her to the edge of the city where stonings occurred, they seemed to be taking her to the center of the village. In the distance, she could see the Mount of Olives, and it perplexed her greatly that they might be taking her some place where even greater indignities awaited her. They slapped her each time she cried out, and by the time they got her to the temple, her tears had dried out.

As they continued to drag her and run their hands over her body, she could hear the powerful voice of a teacher echoing through the main sanctuary of the temple. When they got close enough to make enough ruckus so that all would notice her, they increased their violence against her solely for the effect. A great hush grew over those who were assembled to hear the Teacher, and even he grew still and quiet. They threw her at his feet, and she stayed there for some time, afraid to move.

"Master," she heard the Pharisees and scribes as they addressed him, "this woman was taken in adultery, in the very act."[56]

Jesus knelt down to the woman who was sprawled lengthwise at his feet. He lifted her face gently so that she could see his face, and one look into his eyes did it all.

Her face was streaked and dirty, and her hair had been pulled from the roots in thatches. She had not been afforded the dignity of dressing completely, and the garment pulled around her left much of her body uncovered. As Jesus lifted the woman and helped her to a sitting position, he reached around his neck, and with one swift motion pulled his mantle from his shoulders. He draped his mantle around the woman with such love and tenderness, that for a moment, she forgot why she was there. He then extended his hands and lifted her to her feet, as one might a queen. As Dunastes stood and observed the entire event, he thought of how ironic it was that they would bring one they had marked for death to the Savior's feet.

As Jesus stood and walked slowly away from the woman, Dunastes smiled at the move, understanding the Son of God's strategy.

Not to be deterred, one of the more vocal of the mob pointed at her and continued, "Now, Moses in the law commanded us that such a guilty wretch as this should be stoned. But what do you say should be done with her?"

Jesus looked at each of them as if each man stood alone and read their hearts. The look he gave each of them was piercing, and for a moment, each man felt as if this Jesus knew their most private secrets.

---

[56] John 8:3-11

Jesus, of course, knew that this was not about the woman; this was a setup to get him. He moved a little further away from the woman, increasing the distance between them. Dunastes moved in and stood with a garrison of angels to encircle the woman from further harm. Not one more hand would be laid on her that day.

What the law actually stated was that for the crime of adultery, it was the man who was to take the first stoning, with his lover in tow. When it comes to setups, however, laws and principles are always temporarily suspended. This setup had been contrived for weeks in secret, and a great deal of money had exchanged hands to bring it to fruition. The conspirators had listened to the teachings of Jesus very closely and were outraged that the people considered him the long-awaited Messiah who would save Israel from her enemies.

He had done many miracles and effected many cures, and the sway he held over the people, was in their opinion, nothing short of blasphemous. He openly and flagrantly violated the teachings of the Torah and had on many occasions insulted them by calling them "children of the devil" and "whitened sepulchers." They believed that his very presence among the people incited sedition, and they were not about to sacrifice their hard-won liberty for an unlearned Nazarene. But they needed something meatier to charge him with, and they saw that to entrap him most effectively, they would have to get him to speak openly against the Mosaic Law.

Inexplicably, and without so much as an acknowledgement of what they said, Jesus stooped and began writing on the ground with his finger. The woman felt an unusual calm as she watched, totally unaware of the host of angels who were on special assignment to protect her. One of the angels held her in his arms to comfort her, while another bathed her face in oil. Most of the humans who stood by did not see the change because their eyes were on Jesus. But some did and were baffled by the great beauty of her once stained and tear-streaked face. They were looking at the glory with veiled eyes, but they thought they were looking at her.

As they continued their verbal attack against the woman, Jesus ignored them and seemed preoccupied with the lettering he was etching on the ground.

As the woman watched him, puzzled, she couldn't help wondering to herself, *Why is Jesus writing on the ground?*

The more he wrote, the more her accusers kept up their recitation of an abridged portion of the Mosaic Law.

Just as suddenly as he had knelt, he stood and faced them. "He who is without sin among you, you be the first to cast a stone at her," Jesus responded.

And then, without waiting for them to say anything or do anything, once again, he stooped down on the ground, and this time, he appeared to draw symbols and moderated letters. The woman studied him closely, and puzzled over what a strange man he was, for no one could read words that had been written on the ground. Of course, what she couldn't see was that he was not writing for mortals made of flesh and blood. He was writing for the innumerable cloud of witnesses who could decipher the finger of God.[57]

Every man who stood there, no matter his role or title, was immediately pricked in their conscience as they thought of the sins each was guilty of—some punishable by the same laws that they now stood misquoting. Each began, from the eldest to the youngest, to leave one by one. As they left, they looked furtively one to another, wondering who would be responsible for making sure the woman got stoned. Each decided for himself to err on the side of self-preservation. When they were gone, the woman looked around afraid to feel relief. From her human vantage point, only she and Jesus were left standing there, but actually, there were more than ten thousand spectators, besides.

---

[57] 1 John 2:2

When Jesus first stooped, he began enumerating the woman's sins one by one. She was a liar, she was a thief, and no doubt, she was a fornicator and an adulteress. She was also willful, she was bitter, she was often disobedient, and she was always getting in the middle of whatever the newest mess was in town. She was a busybody, she was a tattler, she was too quick to speak, and was always the first to run and tell what she had heard. The list went on and on. The unseen host stood watching, and some of the devils who were her biggest agitators were also her worst critics. When Jesus thought to leave a sin off of the list, they would goad him into including it.

When the list was done, and he stood and faced her accusers to challenge the innocent to throw the first stone, it was when he stooped the second time that caused the greatest stirring in the crowd of witnesses. This time, and with the same finger, he first began to make symbols indicating that each sin on the list he would now cover for her, thus freeing her of the guilt of her past. Then, with the same finger, and to a now hushed unseen host, he began to write a promissory note to the Father. It read thusly, "Father, I know that this woman is guilty of many sins, and that her just dessert is death. But she is the reason that I have come. Today, I cover this woman, and I cancel every debt she owes. I thank you, Father, that you and I are one, and that you hear me when I pray. For her sake, I ask you to accept me in her place—to take my life that she may live. And Father, I promise you, that one day soon, I will not just cover her sin, but I will cleanse her every wit."[58]

When Jesus stood up the final time and found each of her accusers now gone, the woman's fresh tears of gratitude brought great joy to his heart as well. She was not just a caught woman, but she was the kind of woman who was always entangled by the issues of a woman's heart. Today, she was free. She had never felt safe with a man in all of her life, but today, she met one who would be faithful and true, and never leave her, nor forsake her. Not ever.

---

[58] Ephesians 2:5-8

"Woman, where are those who brought you here to accuse you? Is there not a man left who will condemn you?" Jesus spoke to the woman in a gentle, but firm voice, and turned and pointed with his hands to indicate that none were left.

She thought the flourish of his hands was for effect and to indicate the empty hall where they stood. In actuality, he meant it for the absence of the devils that stood accusing her as well. The tears streamed down her face, and she swallowed hard to find her voice. A nagging thought tried to drag her head down in shame, but Dunastes cupped her chin in his hand and lifted it to the Son of God.

She found herself smiling at him and answered in a soft voice of repentance, "No man, Lord, not one."

Jesus moved gently to the woman and replaced his hand over that of Dunastes. He looked the woman in the eye, knowing that he would see her again and wanting her to always remember that his eyes would be upon her in the days ahead and even through to her old age.

"Neither do I condemn thee. Go, and sin no more!"

When the Savior[59] spoke the words, a power unknown to the woman hit her, and she almost lost her balance. Jesus caught her before she fell and steadied her so that she could breathe in new and abundant life. When she walked out of the temple that day as a changed woman, she also left as a worshipper of the God-man named Jesus.[60]

She had heard that he would be in town at the house of his good friend, Simon the leper. Before Jesus healed the man, all who feared the contagion of his disease shunned him. After his healing, he had been declared clean by the priests, but the label still stuck. He knew

---

[59] Hebrews 1:3-4
[60] Acts 10:43

well what it meant to be ostracized and detested for a state over which he had no control. He would forever be an advocate for people less fortunate than he...but that didn't include women.

When the woman finally arrived at his gates, she did not knock to enter. Jesus sat in the midst of the small group of male guests at supper and knew she was coming before she left her house that morning. He looked up when she entered, and she was momentarily stunned to see that he seemed to be expecting her. The disciples were beside themselves with the offense of her presence, and Jesus turned his genuine concern to Simon the leper for a moment—the man looked like he had imbibed a camel.

She stepped over Simon Peter who tried to run interference, nearly knocked John's wine goblet out of his hand as he tried an elbow maneuver, and she accidentally shoved Andrew in the head because he refused to move. She stepped on the toes of Matthew because he extended his leg to trip her, and without an ounce of grace, she kicked Thomas in the shins because he grabbed her by the hem of her skirts. When she finally got to Jesus, she felt that she had body slammed a whole militia. The Savior, on his part, and because he knew the solemn purpose of her visit, had to work extra hard to choke back laughter.

She reached under her mantle and produced a most elegant alabaster bottle, etched with fine engravings in silver and pearl. She bowed her head for a moment as she stood just behind Jesus and wept freely over the one and only man who had ever loved her unconditionally. As an act of pure worship, she broke the seal on the beautiful and costly bottle and began to pour the spikenard upon the Savior's head. The perfumed aroma filled the house where they were seated, and there was an anointing on her ministry service that silenced the mouth of every critic. Simon Peter started to say something, but the virtue of the act stilled his tongue. Only Judas Iscariot had the audacity to speak.

After the woman had anointed the Savior with oil that she purchased with money from her last prized possession, she knelt at his feet to worship him and began to wipe his feet with her hair. At first, the disciples nourished a prejudice because of her courage, but then, they took note of his response. The oil seemed to have the affect of a healing balm, and they were surprised to see him begin to weep.

"What purpose has been gained by wasting such a precious ointment?" cried Judas who was livid because of the woman's lack of restraint. "This ointment could have been sold for a great deal of money and given to help the poor."

Satan stood close to Judas guiding his words, but not even the other disciples were impressed by his newfound philanthropy.

"Why are you harassing the woman? Leave her alone!" shouted Jesus to the stunned group of men and devils. "Can't any of you see that her motive for coming was to minister to me? You will always have poor folks that need your sacrificial giving, but I will not always be with you!"

He looked around momentarily frustrated with his disciples, but also seeing in the moment an opportunity to teach them something that they would need in the days ahead.

"In that this woman has poured this ointment on my Body, she did it for my burial. And I tell you a truth," Jesus stated as he lifted the woman from his feet, "verily, I say unto you, wherever this great gospel is preached in the whole world, what this woman has done here today shall be told and retold for a memorial to her."

It would be sometime later when the disciples were changed men that they would look back on this hour as apostles and marvel to themselves at the wonder of it all. This woman, in effect, had stepped into the role of a high priest, anointed the head and feet of the Lord, and in so doing, ushered him into his final hour. As time would tell, there was another morning coming when other women would find themselves at the tomb for the purpose of anointing his body for burial, and he would be gone.[61]

Several hours later, when Jesus would find himself in the agony of Gethsemane,[62] the medicinal affect of the oil that the woman had poured on his Body and soaked into his pores would continue to minister to him in his darkest hour. Dunastes looked on in a rare moment of sorrow. The passion of the Christ was soon to begin at the hands of the vilest of human men. Ironically, and as history would tell, it had been a powerful and singular act by a woman that most prepared him.

---

[61] Matthew 28:1-4
[62] Luke 22:44

Chapter 13: Bruised Heel

The mood in the heavens was one of melancholy and poignancy this night, because the Son of God had been betrayed and taken captive by evil men. God's Archangel, Prince Michael, had called for all of the arch commanders to a general assembly, and each called for the lieutenants and rulers under them as well. Prince Michael knew that many of the angels might be tempted to disobey God's commands concerning Jesus and decided to keep his top commanders in check as a way of checking the others. Dunastes had long dreaded this moment, and now, after more than several centuries, it had finally come.

As Michael and his commanders sped through dominions and kingdoms to get to the Earth where the beating of Jesus was taking place, they went directly to the temple where Jesus now stood before the Sanhedrin. Multitudes of the angelic host were there on special commission by the arch commanders, but Dunastes and Rhoomai saw that it was necessary to signal for several garrisons to stand down. They noticed that as Jesus was slapped and spat upon by the Roman soldiers, the agitation in the angelic ranks grew stronger.

"Prophesy unto us," the chief priests yelled at Jesus, "who was it who just slapped you?"

At this, they all made great merriment and pummeled him the more. Dunastes nodded to Chrioni and Rhoomai, indicating that he could take the sight of it no more.

As he made his way away from the temple mount in the darkness, he could see Simon Peter crouched before a makeshift stove, talking in an agitated voice to a young woman. Their voices grew louder as they argued, and Dunastes walked toward them with his eye on a large bird nearby called a cock. He knew that Peter had one more denial to go before the prophetic words of Jesus would come quickly upon him.

"I swear to you, I do not know him!" spat Peter as he argued with her about his association with Jesus.

Others who stood by entered the debate and began to accost him as well.

One yelled, pointing at him, "Someone seize this man. I have seen him in the company of Jesus many times, and I'm telling you, for sure, he is one of them. His own dialect gives him away!"

At this, Peter began cursing and swearing, saying, "I tell you, I don't know this man!"

As the cock began to crow, the words of Jesus came back to him, "Before the cock shall crow, you will deny me three times."[63] At the memory, Peter took off running.

Dunastes could move faster than Peter because he was an angel with wings, but keeping up with Peter on foot was no joy ride in the park. As Peter ran, he ran in agony. Never again in all of his life would he ever experience the pain he felt right now. Earlier that evening, along with the others, he loudly declared that he would rather die than forsake Jesus. He had not only just denied him, but swore it with an oath. His tears burned like hot steel, but he tasted his own blood as well. Tree branches and limbs thrashed his face, creating cuts and bruises, but he kept running because he felt that if he ran hard and fast enough, he might finally come to the edge of the world itself.

Dunastes was right behind him. Up ahead was a ford adjacent to the main road, and just beyond its shore was a garrison of devils waiting to claim Peter's soul at the moment of his death. Dunastes was expecting them and drew his sword for the fight that lie ahead. As Peter ran blindly, Dunastes ran with vision and caught thousands of them with the edge of his sword before they ever knew what hit them.

---

[63] Matthew 26:74,75

His double-edged gladius met steel with steel, and as he swung it like a gigantic lathe, the lightning strikes from the blows burned permanent gouges in the ground. The stalwart champion drove back several hosts of demons alternating between his sword in one hand and his pugio in the other. As he gathered himself up, he spread his wings like a great eagle in flight and prepared himself for the next assault. He descended upon a second wave of fallen angels with such ferocious accuracy that he routed them before they had time to react.

Several demonic powers ran straight for him, swinging wildly and determined to overwhelm the enormous commander. He had the greater advantage with his expansive wingspan and created carnage among the devil warriors. But the fight was far from over. Peter kept running, and Dunastes stayed with him and fought devils along the way. Initially, he favored the gladius and did tremendous damage with his fighting hand. As the devils swarmed as thick as flies, he found himself fighting with both his sword and his pugio at once.

The sky lit up with the glory of the heavens, and he felt momentarily relieved when he saw an innumerable company of angelic soldiers descend all at once. Some were infantry, but most were mounted on horses, and they touched down with their swords in motion. Now that help had arrived, Dunastes folded his wings, went back to the ground, and kept running with Peter on foot. Often, Peter would stumble hard, not knowing that the rock which pierced his skin was actually intended to kill him. Had he been able to see into the spirit realm, he would have seen the gigantic hand of Dunastes deflect the rock to keep it from its intended mark. Peter kept on running.

As Dunastes looked to the night sky, he could see the formation of other demonic garrisons gathering themselves in battle line formation as they prepared to make a second strike. He was waiting and ready. The first line of devil warriors tried to flank from the forward position rather than the rear, but he found it easy to move them back by running straight toward the centerline of their assault. When they surrounded him, he pulled both the pugio and gladius and fought them with both hands. Peter kept running, and Dunastes stayed with him.

At the moment of the third wave of attack, Peter was exhausted, but Dunastes was in his best element. A mighty force of angels sent by Rhoomai met the third contingent of devils, and before the strike could even get underway, Dunastes had driven more than half of them back into the darkness. He kept watching the sky, hoping Satan would appear. But Satan was taking care of other more important things, like helping Judas tie a noose around his own neck. When the knot was tight enough but Judas faltered momentarily, Satan kicked him from the cliff he was perched on, and he fell headlong, breaking his body apart on impact. Arch commander Chrioni was there to witness it, and it was the saddest thing he would ever see.

Peter wept bitterly for more than an hour. His anguish was the soul-cry of a man in torment, and the sound of it moved the most robust of God's angels to compassion. The angels of God knelt around him to protect him with their wings, but Dunastes watched the sky, hoping for just one more wave of devils. The fighting was good that night for practice, but he felt that just a few more hordes of them would help him correct a flaw in his fighting hand.

It didn't take long for the report to get back to Satan that his best garrisons had lost Peter. He was livid at the news. Instead of sending an emissary, he would face Dunastes himself. The angelic champion was waiting patiently for him and hoping with everything within him that he would bring more of his best reinforcements. As they waited, Peter was inconsolable and at several points was close to hysteria. The angels of God formed a tight circle around him, while others stood with swords ready to move the fight for his soul to the next level.

Satan knew that although Jesus would be dead soon, he could not win unless the disciples were dead, too. He had studied and listened to Jesus very carefully and had heard his words about establishing his Father's kingdom on Earth. Satan laughed to himself. This was some kingdom he had established! In the morning, the plot to kill him would be carried out in a gory mess, and he would be there to witness every glorious moment of it. His use of parables got on Satan's nerves, and his reference to eternal salvation for men who were mortal perplexed him to no end.

He could hardly wait until Jesus was dead, so that he could go and contend for the body. Satan felt certain that the ultimate mission of Jesus was to re-take dominion of the Earth, and by taking possession of his Body, he could desecrate it in the grave. He had heard many references to what Jesus referred to as the gospel and was only loosely concerned about the multitude of other disciples Jesus called, other than the twelve. He knew that if push came to shove, once his closest disciples were dead, his teachings would end as so many had before him. With the events that were soon to occur, he felt comfortable that if Jesus was who he really said he was, he had failed miserably.

Before the night was done, he knew that it was absolutely critical that the twelve had to die. He had one down, but there were eleven more to go, and he was determined that not even Arch Commander Dunastes would stop him.

Finding Dunastes was easy. The arch commander lit up the eastern sky with the glory of God that was upon him.

"The man, Peter, belongs to me!" cried Satan. He was in a foul mood and was not there to mince words with Dunastes.

"He is mine! Jesus has lost! I am still the Son of the Morning, and the Bright and Morning Star. He has failed in his mission—the kingdoms of the world belong to me! Throw your allegiance to me, all ye angels of God, and I will give you great power and authority in this world and in that which is to come!" bellowed Satan.

Dunastes remained surprisingly calm, but the other angels began to move toward him for a fight. Dunastes stepped out to block their progress, for he knew that this was neither the time nor the season to wage war with him, although it was very tempting. Peter, by now, had slept fitfully through the night and would never know the details of the fight for his soul until the day that he would be told in Paradise.

Satan and Dunastes began to move, circling each other as if to spar. Each had a weapon in his hand, and both had a dangerous look to the eyes. Dunastes was creeping past the line of no return, when Prince Michael himself came upon the scene. His arrival brought a surge of excitement to the battleground, and the hosts parted company and saluted in reverence. Satan was having none of it.

"The man, Peter, belongs to me, Michael!" bellowed Satan. "I have a right to his soul; he has denied any allegiance to Jesus, and he now belongs to me![64] You will release him into my custody or face the consequences for your defiance!"

Michael peered at Satan, amazed at the threat. As Michael stepped up next to his arch commander, he could see that his arrival was not a moment too late. He nodded for Dunastes to stand down with his weapon and was pleased to see that Peter was secure.

The arch commanders who accompanied Michael were less reserved than Dunastes, and momentarily, the archangel was distracted by their hostility. Some of them had come from the governor's common hall and had witnessed the Roman soldiers strip Jesus of his clothing and place a scarlet robe upon him to mock him. They wept the tears of angels, as they stood helpless to defend him.

With bowed heads and heavy hearts, they watched as the soldiers platted a crown of thorns and then shoved it down upon the crown of his head. The blood ran in a steady stream down his beard. They put a reed in his right hand and bent their knees to mock him, saying, "Hail, King of the Jews!" It was all that the arch commanders could do to

---

[64] Luke 22:31-32

contain themselves, as they stood watching the soldiers take turns spitting in the face of the Son of God.[65] They took the reed from the hand of Jesus and beat him about his head, until his eyes were swollen shut from the razor-thin bruising. When Michael called for several of them to follow him, it was not a minute too soon. Just as they were leaving, they looked back to see the Savior being led out to be hanged on a tree.

"Why have you come here, Prince Michael? You break the laws of heaven! What rights have you to be here? The man, Peter, belongs to me! He is mine to sift as wheat!" hissed Satan.

"Sheath your weapon, Devil!" ordered the gigantic archangel who towered several feet above Satan's head. "Sheath it now, before I loose my commanders to give you a taste of what you just did to the man, Judas!"

This time, it was Prince Michael who hissed at Satan, and it was more than a threat. Dunastes was hoping that Satan would refuse. Rhoomai was thinking that they should cut him and repent about it later. Chrioni already had a hand on his sword.

"You have won nothing!" cried Prince Michael. "This is the aftermath of Eden, Devil. One day, you will pay for your rebellion in heaven, but today, you will pay for what you did to the first Adam. The Son of God has already prayed for Peter that his faith would not fail in this darkest hour. It is because of the prayers of the Savior that we have come to fight for his life. He will live and not die! He will never belong to you!"

Michael waxed eloquent as he spoke, and his arch commanders settled down. There was too much at stake here than just winning a brawl. They knew that soon the Son of God would rejoin them in all of his majesty and glory, and that one day, he would sit at the head of

---

[65] Mark 15:18-20

God's armies. They longed for that day and knew that they must maintain order and discipline.

Satan literally turned red with rage. The sight of Prince Michael and the greatest of God's angelic champions blocking his path to a mortal man were almost more than he could handle. He needed Peter desperately. He thought about the time that he used Peter to rebuke Jesus for talking about death, and remembered how it startled him when Jesus looked past Peter and saw him. He thought about what a big mouth Peter was, and how his quick temper and impetuousness had always been so easy to manipulate. To have such a big quarry slip from his grip was a major coup for the Lord's camp. As he stood weighing his options, he rolled back his head and roared until the ground shook. It woke Peter up at the same time that Jesus was dragging a wooden cross up Golgotha's hill.

As Peter looked around, his body aching from the previous night's events, he wondered if it all had been but a bad dream. Something had awakened him, and he shook himself to make sure that he was still alive. He had intended to kill himself, and momentarily, the thought came to him that perhaps now would be a good time to finish what he had planned. What he could not know was that at the moment he awoke, garrisons of angels including Satan and Prince Michael all turned to look at him at once. It was a strange sight with so many devils and angels gathered calmly together in one place.

Satan knew that legally, he could not touch Peter. With great malice and indignity, he turned and nodded to his champions to leave. The hordes of dark powers and demons gathered in clouds of dust and turned to depart without a sound. Finally, Satan himself backed away reluctantly and left in a great flourish.

But then, after he had walked only a few steps, he turned and faced Michael once more. "This is not over. The man, Peter, belongs to me. I can take him now or take him another day, but I will have him." With that, the Devil turned and walked away.

Several angelic lieutenants helped Peter up from the ground and spoke comfort to him. Not seeing them with his natural eyes, Peter waved them away, refusing to be comforted. As he remembered his treachery from the night before, it reduced him to tears, and he sat once again and rocked his head in his hands. He couldn't stop remembering, and so many things crowded his mind for attention. He felt like a man going insane.

There was something that kept nagging at the corners of his mind, and he reached out to grab the words like a desperate man wanting to be saved. It was something that Jesus once spoke to him, and now he sat savoring those words like morsels to a dying soul. There was an occasion when Jesus posed what the disciples thought was a rhetorical question to them. He wanted to know what the rumors were about his identity.

Andrew answered first and said, "Some say you are John the Baptist, others say you are the Prophet Elijah, and still others say that you must be Jeremiah or one of the other prophets."

All of the other disciples stood nodding their assent.

"And whom do all of you say that I am?" queried Jesus.

They looked nervously from one to the other. They were so accustomed to giving the wrong response that they generally looked to Peter to answer for them all so that he could be the one to put his foot in his mouth.

True to form, Peter stepped forward as the others held their peace and without blinking stated, "Thou art the Christ, the Son of the living God."[66] There was an anointing on it when he said it, and all of the disciples felt the change when it came upon him.

Jesus reacted just as fervently, "You are blessed, Simon Barjona, because flesh and blood men did not reveal my identity unto you, but

---

[66] Matthew 16:13-17

143

my Father who is in heaven could have been the only One who told you. I tell you a truth—you have always been identified as Peter the large rock. But I am also a rock—a massive rock on which you can lean and depend. And upon the foundation of this revelation that you have just been given, I will build a church that the gates of hell shall not prevail against."[67]

The memory of the words warmed Peter like a blanket, and the tears that he now shed began to wash his soul. Although he could not erase the deep remorse he felt at forsaking the one he loved more than words could say, somehow the words that he spoke about Peter's future came back now to keep him from ending his own life. He knew that Jesus would by now be probably dead—death by Roman crucifixion was both gruesome and bloody, and he realized now that the torture must have lasted through most of the night. He wanted to go to Jesus, his Master, but the realization that all had been lost was more than he could bear.

As he sat rocking himself, trying to maintain a grip on his own mind, his thoughts turned to anger. He had seen Jesus save many. He had even walked with him on the sea.[68] If indeed he were the Son of God, why didn't he save himself from being taken? Peter didn't understand and kept playing many things that Jesus had said over and over again in his mind.

The thoughts began to torture his mind, and before he knew it, he was running again. He ran this time toward the village of his Galilean birth, wanting only to run as far as he could from the failed mission of a Man he thought was surely the Christ. There was nothing that mattered to him at that moment—not his wife, not his children…not anything. As he ran, the angels ran with him, and it was actually a good thing for him to keep running. Eventually, he was going to run out, and when he did, his faith would never fail him again, and he would in turn strengthen his brothers.

---

[67] Matthew 16:18
[68] Matthew 14:29

Section Three

It Is Finished

Chapter 14: Who Rolled Away the Stone?

"My lord, at the moment that he died, the earth trembled, and the sun hid its face in shame. Surely, My lord, this man was the Son of God indeed!" It was the centurion who had stood at the foot of the cross who spoke to Pontius Pilate about the death of the Christ.

"What did he say before he died?" asked Pilate, remembering the bothersome night visions of his wife.

The centurion peered at him and looked away. The final words of Jesus had been almost too much for him to bear.

Hesitating, the centurion began, "My lord, there was one of the two thieves on either side of him who began to curse his day, but he calmly ignored his words. One said to him, 'If you are really the Son of God, save us and save yourself,' but the other rebuked the first who spoke, and to the Christ he said, 'Remember me when you have come into your Kingdom.' The Christ then turned upon his cross and said to him, ignoring the other, 'Today, you shall be with me in paradise.'"

For a moment, the centurion grew silent, as both he and the governor momentarily envied the promise given to the thief.

"Say on," encouraged Pilate for he was anxious to hear it all.

"The chief priests of the Jews are a brutish bunch, my lord. They had no pity on him as he suffered. They yelled at him, 'You saved others; now save yourself if you are really the Son of God. Come down from the cross. Prove to us that you are who you say you are!'[69] The King of the Jews then did an extraordinary thing, my lord. He turned to the heavens and spoke to One he addressed as his Father, saying, 'Father, forgive them for they know not what they do.'"

---

[69] Mark 15:23-32

Pilate looked at him in disbelief for he was personally acquainted with the gory mess of crucifixions and was shocked at the report that Jesus could even speak after such torture. Pilate nodded for him to continue.

"Then, my lord," the centurion said with a quiet hush, "after he was offered wine to dull his pain, he spoke words which are most difficult to understand."

Pilate looked at him in agitation, as the words of the centurion were filled with suspense.

"What was it that he said, tell me, what were his last words before he died?" At this point, Pilate was on the edge of his seat.

"My lord," the centurion began again in halting speech, "he said, 'It is finished!' and then he died."[70]

Both Pilate and the centurion locked eyes in silence; each wondered to himself what the strange words could mean. The centurion nodded to the governor, signaling the end of his accounting. After he stood for several moments and Pilate had neglected to speak, he cleared his throat loudly, suspecting that Pilate had forgotten that he was standing there.

Startled, Pilate looked up at him, embarrassed. He had indeed forgotten that the centurion was standing there.

"Darius," Pilate addressed the high commander, "have you delivered the body to Joseph of Arimathea?"

The centurion nodded that he had. Momentarily, Pilate got lost again in his thoughts.

---

[70] Mark 15:37-39

"My lord, is there more?" queried the tired centurion; he was eager to get some rest. Though he had been a soldier all of his life, this killing of the man called Jesus was by far the most unsettling. He stood there, remembering the crazed look in the eyes of a soldier called Brutus who had been the one who had driven the nails into the palms and ankles of the Christ. Darius saw Brutus that morning before answering Pilate's summons and was stunned by the soldier's deterioration. The crucifixion would haunt Brutus for the balance of his days, and the centurion would one day stand as a witness to his suicide. As irony would have it, he would be buried in the Potter's Field right next to a soul named Judas.

Pilate looked up, interrupting the centurion's thoughts, and spoke once more. You could tell that the events of the past day or two had taken its toll on the senior statesman. "What do these want from me who stand outside my chambers?"

There had been a large contingent of chief priests and Pharisees waiting patiently for an audience with Pilate.

"My lord, I do not know, but perhaps, they realize their mistake to loose Barabbas.[71] I am told that he is already at work to plan a new revolt among the people."

Pilate threw up his hands in exasperation at the news.

"Bring them in!" Pilate ordered.

When the whole mob of them entered Pilate's chambers, it was the high priest who took center stage.

"My lord," started the centurion, "do I have your permission to take my leave?"

---

[71] Matthew 27:19-26

The high priest interjected quickly, "Governor, do not permit him to leave. If it pleases my lord, our petition involves the Praetorian Guard."

Greatly put off by the high priest's presumption, the centurion glared at him.

"Say on," was the response from Pilate, seeing the centurion's displeasure and nodding his agreement that he should remain.

"My lord," the high priest began, as they all gathered around him as if he spoke with one voice, "Sir, may we remind you that the deceiver told us while he was yet alive that after three days, he would rise again. Command that the sepulcher be made sure until the third day be past. We believe that his disciples intend to take his body under the cover of darkness and make claim to the people that he has risen from the dead. If we allow their plot to move forward, the last error shall be worse than the first."[72]

Though Pilate felt that they were pushing the envelope with their presumption, their words held logic. He wanted this entire matter, including the memory of the one who claimed to be the Christ, put behind him as quickly as possible.

He nodded in agreement to their request and then turned to give the centurion the new command. "You will provide a watch as so requested; these will go with you to ensure that it meets their demands." The last words were spoken with a good bit of acid. He wanted this bunch out of his sight as quickly as possible.

They departed quickly to the tomb and where the Body of Jesus had been laid to rest. The centurion ordered a small garrison of soldiers to set a watch over the tomb for three days. As a final measure and to secure the tomb, his soldiers rolled a great stone

---

[72] Matthew 27:63-66

sealing the mouth. It weighed several tons and took more than thirty soldiers to move it—and even that with hooks and chains.

As the centurion gave his final orders and turned to walk away, Satan was having an epiphany of his own.

Satan stood watching the dying of Jesus, anxiously waiting to greet him in the bowels of the Earth. He had several legions ready to put him in chains at his arrival. This time, there would be no fighting, for the angels of God had no license to enter his abode. The Grave belonged exclusively to him, for he had won it fair and square when Adam fell. He felt certain that he was fighting a battle that he would finally win. Finally, all of this would be over, and it would prove to the entire heavenly host and especially to God that he was the one who deserved sonship, for he was victor of all. Of course, he was wrong about that, but he wouldn't know it until he came face to face with Jesus alive in the Grave.

As his devils prompted the soldiers to taunt Jesus, Satan stood there taking everything in and reflecting on the bad, as well as the good. The plan to take the Earth from him by stealth was the worse plan that the fallen angel could imagine. Man was at best, weak and unreliable, and even when Satan sought to use one for his own advantage, the Man could turn on you in a moment and leave you hanging with nothing gained. The Devil hated mankind with a passion and found nothing quite as satisfying as having them blame God for something he took, stole, or killed.

He reminisced about the man, Noah, and how much God looked to his three sons Ham, Japheth, and Shem to provide heirs after the flood who would be godly men. Satan nipped that in the bud real quick by having Ham touch his father's nakedness while he was too drunk to know what his son was doing to him in the dark.[73] He thought about Moses and how highly God had thought of him. That one was easy

---

[73] Genesis 9:22-24

enough. His devils worked overtime through the nagging and complaining of the people during their exodus from Egypt, and in no time, they got Moses angry and disobedient enough to strike the rock at Horeb. His mind went to Deborah and Barak, and for a moment, he bristled at the memory of Sisera dying at the hand of a wretched woman.[74] She drove a nail through his temple while he lay on the floor, sipping milk.

It wasn't easy to think about the man, King David, but then, he remembered what a triumph it was when he got him to kill Uriah so that he could have Bathsheba for his wife. It made him sick to think about Samuel, but then, he remembered what pawns the prophet's sons had been. He thought about the prophets Isaiah, Ezra, Elijah, and Nehemiah. The whole lot of them had been a royal thorn in his side. King Saul started out being a threat to his plan for Israel, but then, he got him where he wanted him when he sought counsel from the witch at Endor. Solomon had been an easy target by ensnaring him with women, but then, when he asked for wisdom to lead God's people, he ruined everything with his musings. The prophets Jeremiah, Ezekiel, and Hosea were the bane of his existence, and Jonah messed everything up when he said yes to Nineveh instead of just drowning.

The whole sorry lot of mankind, while useful for wars, mayhem, and spreading error and lawlessness, was more trouble to manage than Satan felt they were worth. He peered up at the cross once more. He wanted badly for Jesus to finish dying so that he could finish off his disciples as well.

There would be a gospel, all right, Satan thought, *but not the one that Jesus thought would mean much to anybody who would believe in a dead hero.*

---

[74] Judges 5:26

When he finally cried, "It is finished!"[75] Satan sighed a sigh of relief. In the greatest miscalculation since his fall, he called for his powers of darkness to all assemble as one with him against Jesus. They all descended into the nether regions of the Earth and followed close on his heels to the point of his death. When they saw that he was alone, they could hardly hide their jubilation. He was dressed in no armor and brandished no sword, and for once, his angels would not be able to come to his rescue.

"You have lost!" Satan screamed at him as he faced him in the Grave. The fallen angel could hardly contain himself. "You could have thrown your allegiance to me, and I would have rewarded you with the kingdoms of my world," Satan lied.

"But now, you belong to me, and I shall make you pay for what you have done to me. Put him in chains!" Satan bellowed, now beside himself with rage.

As the devils approached Jesus carrying a massive chain with which to bind him, Jesus made an aggressive advance toward them rather than backing away from them.

All at once, he snatched the chain out of the dark ruler who stood before him and squeezed the rivets with such an amazing power that it shattered at their feet. They all peered at him, stunned.

"You are dead," cried Satan, "you have no power or authority here, and you are now constrained to this underworld with me."

This time, the Lord was the one who advanced toward Satan with a sword which proceeded from his Mouth. "No, you are the one who has lost, Satan, for I am here to bruise your head!"

---

[75] John 19:30

The sword that came out of His mouth was a double-bladed sword that cut asunder every spirit it touched. It seemed to move with a life-energy its own. Satan fell back from the force of it and soon fled into the outer darkness leaving his devils to face Jesus alone. He took captivity captive[76] with the sword of his Mouth and threw open the doors of the prisoners held there behind bars. He preached to the righteous dead who were bound there and gave eternal life to those who had longed for his coming. As a last act, he took the sting out of death. He was there for three days in the belly of the Earth, and when he ascended, he held the keys to the Grave in his hand. He spoiled principalities and powers and made a show of them openly, and one day soon, the last enemy he would destroy would be death.[77]

When he rose from the dead and first appeared to the woman, Mary of Magdala,[78] he had not yet ascended to his Father's throne. When he whispered the woman's name as she stood weeping at the empty tomb, legions of his angels surrounded him for gladness.

"Mary," he whispered again, "do not weep for it is I!"

When Mary looked up and mistook him for a stranger, he once again called her by name. As she ran to touch him, he drew back from her hand and assured her of his identity as her Lord. Dunastes, Rhoomai, Chrioni, and the Lord's host stood round about him with the archangels, Gabriel and Michael. He had promised them that the Grave could not hold him, and that he would rise again with all power in his hand. But it was Mary who had the greater shock, for just as he had withdrawn from her touch, she saw the holes in his hands where the nails had been driven through.

---

[76] Ephesians 4:8-10
[77] Colossians 2:14-15
[78] Mark 16:9

"Mary," cried Jesus to her, "go tell my disciples that you have seen me, and that I am alive forevermore!"[79]

By the time the centurion got to the tomb of Jesus and got the dreaded report from his garrison stationed there, the scene was one of chaos. He was told that women had been there first to prepare the body for burial, and that when they got there and found the tomb of the Christ empty, save his grave clothes and head napkin, that they ran to tell Jesus' disciples. The soldiers who stood there readied themselves to be killed for the loss of the Body, but the centurion was willing to spare them until he had audience with Pilate.

With haste, the centurion made his way to the governor's hall, trying desperately to think of the right words that would save the lives of his soldiers and perhaps his own life as well. When he was summoned before Pilate, he walked in quickly and saluted him with dread.

"Darius!" thundered Pilate, for he had already received the early report from the Pharisees and the high priests.

"Speak!"

The centurion met his gaze and in halting speech shared the facts as he knew them. He claimed that the soldiers whom he had assigned to the watch were the best of his legion. They were battle-trained soldiers and the cream of the crop, but Darius took a great chance in defending their honor.

"Where were they when the Body was taken? Are you telling me they all forsook their post?"

The centurion could see that Pilate was breathing hard, and he remembered how he had washed his hands of the blood of Jesus a few

---

[79] Revelation 1:16-18

days before. The sight of it came back now to haunt Darius, and he wondered if the bloodstains of Jesus would ever wash free of his own.

"My lord, they were asleep," was the flat response of the commander. Pilate stared at him speechless and unable to speak. "My lord, we believe that the disciples of Jesus came during the slumber of my soldiers and secreted away the Body just as the Jews warned us."

For a moment, Pilate could but stare at his top commander in disbelief. Then, he leaned forward and posed as a final question, "If it happened as you have said...who rolled away the stone?"[80]

---

[80] Mark 16:3,4

Chapter 15: The Church

Ruth and Naomi sat with a group of angels who just returned from a conflict on the decaying, now rancid Earth. That was odd…they weren't as talkative about their bold adventure as they normally were. The two women had always welcomed—even relished—the loud, boisterous retelling of their fights with the princes and demons from the lower heavens. It just wasn't normal for this group to be so sullen. Inevitably, somebody always had to shout for them to please lower their voices.

"Dunastes," she addressed the huge, stalwart angel by his secret name, "What is it? Why are you so quiet tonight?"

The commander stood to his full height and looked down squarely into Naomi's eyes. "Come, and I will show you. I need a backup plan…maybe the two of you can help me."

Naomi and Ruth moved swift as lightning…they had to if they wanted to keep up with this commander who had gained his reputation from freeing the apostles out of many a well-garrisoned jail. As they moved through the earth realms, the two women grew more and more perplexed. The commander seemed to be taking them to a region they had never visited before. They stopped, and the scene that played out before them took Naomi's breath away. Was this really happening?

A group of godly women stood around the bedside of an older woman, whose soot-colored spirit was slowly leaving the old tabernacle of flesh. It sickened Naomi and Ruth to see the merry band of demons who stood wringing their hands in anticipation, waiting for the dying to be done. The lips of hell curled around the feet of the woman, waiting to suck her into its throat.

Ruth screamed at the group of women, in spite of the spirit-world understanding that they could not hear her from the great gulf fixed between them and her.

"Pray!" was the single desperate plea that came forth.

Naomi dropped to her knees where she stood next to Dunastes and began to intercede for the woman herself. It was of no use, and Dunastes sadly grabbed her up again. In this realm, her prayers would only work for believers.

"Listen!" he demanded of her.

One of the women, a minister, said to the near-dead woman, "You'll never be able to abort another innocent baby born into this world—may God have mercy on your soul, sinner."

The old woman slipped a little farther into the netherworld, bound by prison bars. Her time was almost gone.

Another standing close by said, "Your hands are covered with the blood of the innocent.[81] Hell is too good for you."

Dunastes grunted in dismay at the words from these women. He had sent them thinking that they would provide the necessary intercessory prayers he needed to save the soul of the abortionist.[82] They were members of the women's ministry at the church that was adjacent to this woman's house. Although they had been fighting for more than a decade to have this woman ousted from their community, they had never thought of praying for her salvation.[83] The fact that this group whom he had sent was doing just the opposite of what he needed them to do, deeply wounded the angelic champion. Now, he

---

[81] Proverbs 6:16,17
[82] James 5:16-20
[83] James 5:15

would need a back-up plan to save the soul of the abortionist. He needed this group of believers desperately,[84] but they had let him down. If only they could know that there was a pit in the side of hell that was booby-trapped with unspeakable horrors awaiting this woman...if only they knew....

A third woman, spiritually younger than the rest but a believer nonetheless, spoke to the others, "I wish she would just die and be done with it. What's taking her so long to die?"

In truth, the presence of Dunastes was what was holding up matters. In view of the disturbing circumstances before them, his being there was in clear violation of the laws of heaven. With an air of contempt, Dunastes pulled his gladius from its scabbard and pointed it in threatening fashion in the general direction of the unclean spirits that had filled the air at his coming.

They were brazen enough to believe that by circling the lone angelic commander, they could easily rout him and the two unarmed women at his side. They knew that they had a right to be there. On the other hand, without the mysterious interception of prayer,[85] the giant commander of the Lord's hosts had no right to be there. But it wasn't the sword of Dunastes that bugged them the most. It was those two women who were with him who needled them more.

The devils searched their memories, trying to remember the Earth identities of these two. One of the older of the demonic bunch named Bitterness, thought Naomi's face looked awfully familiar, but her change had erased the lines in her soul that would have made it easier for him to remember her. *Forget it*, he thought, *better stay focused.* This Dunastes was known all over the heavens for his ability to literally snatch souls back from the gates of damnation. These

---

[84] Matthew 7:21-23
[85] Philippians 4:6-8

159

captains of the Lord's host, with their flagrant disregard for the rights of devils, got on his nerves!

That was when Ruth got the idea that Dunastes needed. He smiled at the insight she gave him. He was right in guessing that Naomi or Ruth would not only give him a human point of view to his dilemma, but a female's view at that. As she whispered the idea to Dunastes, he made a daring summons to a battalion of his most vicious lieutenants. My Lord, and my God, gasped Naomi, they had witnessed many things, but they had never had the opportunity witness a fight over a soul for themselves.

The demonic host was equally perplexed. They understood the importance of the soul that was fast slipping into eternal damnation before them, but they couldn't understand why these angels were willing to engage them in a cause that was lost. There were no humans who were standing in the gap for this miserable woman. What could the commander gain in a combat for her? Without the human intervention of prayer, a fight would only prolong the moment of her death...nothing more could be gained at this point.

As his angels drew double-edged swords—grinning at the prospect of a fight, Dunastes left the combat in the charge of one of his most trusted lieutenants, Sebazomai. In a twinkling of an eye, he returned the two women quickly into the secure corridors of heaven. Stunned, they watched as he quickly flew away. They asked no questions, for they knew that a soul was at stake.

The angelic captain had no trouble finding the woman he sought. There was a whole host of fierce warrior angels who stood in battle readiness around her. She was nothing great in terms of the way mankind defined *great*, and very few humans in her community had ever set eyes on her, although she walked right past them on a daily basis. She was up to her ears in debt, and by anyone's standard of appearance, she wasn't much to look at. What a shock her fellow humans would have had if they could but know how the angels of God highly esteemed her. They clamored to be the ones selected with the honor to guard her.[86] The demons knew who she was as well and hated her with a passion.

It was the dead of night, and she was fast asleep as Dunastes expected she would be. Dunastes grabbed her by the shoulders and gently pulled her up to a sitting position. Instantly alert, the woman gasped as she caught a glimpse of his divine nature for just a second.

As she looked around trying to adjust her vision and her presence of mind, Dunastes whispered to her, "Pray...pray for the abortionist who drove you to Christ. She is in grave danger of hell fire."

Dalia saw the woman's face as clear as day. As she scrambled out of bed, she stretched prostrate on her face and went into immediate intercession. She was a seasoned veteran in prayer warfare and had always been an interminable thorn in the side of thousands of demons. Her angels pulled their swords from the scabbards, just itching and hoping that some demons would show up to try to stop her. The captain, whose name was Adrian, reached over and touched her, and this gave her added strength for the spiritual battle.

Her soul went into agony for this nameless woman who had performed the abortion on her, which had changed her life. As Dalia entered into the holy place of prayer petitioning God for the salvation of this woman, she remembered how she had fled this woman's house in wretched hopelessness and despair—straight into the path of one of those little Bible-toting street missionaries who always appear to be just a little whacked. The street missionary ministered to her right there on the spot and spoke to her about the steadfast love of Jesus who died for every one of her sins no matter how great. She received Christ into her heart on the promise of the street missionary that there was no sin that God would not forgive her for. Dalia received the forgiveness of God that night and then forgave herself. She had never

---

[86] Acts 10:30,31; Daniel 10:12

looked back to her old life. It was in this manner that she had forged the peculiar bond with the nameless abortionist who had driven her into the arms of Jesus.

In an intense soul-fight of prayer, Dalia warred all night long. Just as the daybreak came, she felt the thing break with the sound of a snap in her spirit. She didn't know how, when, or where—but she knew that the abortionist had been snatched from something dreadful and unspeakable. Every inch of her frame ached and pained her—the battle had been intense. Her head and limbs throbbed as if someone had beaten her with sticks and rocks. She knew what she must do; but it was Adrian who actually whispered the instructions into her spirit.

Quickly, she dressed herself, recalling the address of the abortionist who, with the passage of the years, would have to be an old woman by now. Trusting the leading of the Holy Spirit, she just knew in her spirit that the woman would still live in the same place—she couldn't explain it–she just knew it. As a matter of fact, as she recalled, there was a little sanctified church right next door to the woman's house.

As she made her way through the streets with the urgent conviction in her heart that she must minister Christ to the abortionist right away, what an odd thought came to her mind. *"Thank you for being my backup plan,"* was what she heard whispered in her spirit. Not until she arrived in heaven, which would be soon, would Ruth and Naomi be able to sit with her and explain just what those words meant.

Chapter 16: There Was War in Heaven

More than a thousand arch commanders stood ready with their legions, among them Rhoomai, Chrioni, and Dunastes. At the head of Sabaoth and leading the charge was God's warring archangel, Prince Michael. Although their brilliant standards in crests of gold hues, royal and blue, were raised high at the front lines of the massive columns, on this occasion, they had their battle clothes on. They had been waiting for this fight for centuries, and several of the Old Testament prophets stood with them as excited witnesses.

Dunastes, on his part, could hardly contain himself. That morning when Prince Michael summoned his arch commanders for final examination and to make the final assignments, he called Dunastes out before them all. The stalwart commander moved forward at the nod of Michael, with his heart beating fast. He would finally meet his opponent, Satan, face to face, and didn't care whether his legions moved first or last. He just wanted a single opportunity to meet his ancient adversary toe to toe.

"Commander Dunastes," Michael addressed him before the others.

"Yes, my lord, what is your command?" responded the steely commander with the traditional salute.

"When this battle is over," Michael replied, "and Satan and his powers are driven from the heavens, he will be given limited time to do war with the Church on the Earth.[87] We expect that in a final rage, he will inflict great persecution on mankind because he knows that his time is short."

"When that set time is over," Michael continued to the rapt attention of all those who stood listening, "Yahweh has granted you

---

[87] Revelation 20:1-8

the privilege of being the commander to put him in chains. You and your garrisons will then deliver him to Hell where he will be bound for one thousand years."

Michael's words sent a gasp, and then a hush, through the ranks of the arch commanders who stood eagerly waiting. They had all privately longed for this prize.

The great Commander Dunastes momentarily lowered his head. He was nearly overcome with emotion. Several commanders who just moments before stood shoulder to shoulder with him, sought the approval of Michael to celebrate him. Michael nodded to give them the time. With that, and all at once, the arch commanders surrounded him with noisy rejoicing. Some grabbed him by the shoulders and shook him; others just walked up to him and locked eyes with him with great emotion. Others, who were his closest compatriots, could hardly hold back their tears.

While most spoke few words because the trophy was so great, Rhoomai's words summed it up for them all.

"My friend," the great commander spoke to Dunastes, "when you chain him, whatever you do to get him to yield, do it one more time for me!"

With that, the arch commanders raised a shout so terrible that it shook the temple mount in the Holy City of Jerusalem. Michael stood with a half-smile at the suggestion made by Rhoomai. He planned to get a good one in himself though the final glory would be left to Dunastes.

Michael turned and nodded for the celebration to end with the words, "Game over; let the war begin!"

The commanders turned in great shouting and jubilance, each headed toward the Holy Jerusalem where the pitched battle would take place.

As each arch commander surveyed the massive columns of soldiers that were under their particular command, there was an air of excitement balanced by solemnity, for the battle won here today would end one thing, but begin something else. They waited with swords drawn and shields at their sides. Thousands time ten thousands and thousands mounted garrisons were a terror to look upon, and the infantry which brought up the rear guard was stomping in unison, and the sound of it made the heavens tremble.

All at once, Prince Michael extended his sword to give the signal for the battle, and the great columns, great quiet. Their eyes were on him, and their ears strained to hear the sound of Satan's armies gathering for the battle that they could not win. From Michael's rear, tens of thousands of sentries rode swiftly to announce that the lines of Satan's army were fixed. With that, Archangel Michael yelled for Rhoomai's divisions to lead the charge with the first strike. Rhoomai, in turn, let out a shout so terrible, that it could be heard the full length of Satan's divisions, in number, ten thousand thousands, times ten thousand. Chrioni's massive legions followed him, and then Dunastes, and then the others in swift sequence after him.

There was war in heaven.[88] Michael and his angels fought Satan and his angels, and hordes of the most powerful demons in Satan's kingdom were driven from their ancient strongholds.[89] Some had been principalities, others had been powers, and still others rulers of darkness over nations, governments, philosophies, political systems, beliefs, city states, kings, rulers, presidents, world kingdoms, religions, institutions, dictators, fraternities, and schools.

---

[88] Revelation 12:7-11
[89] Revelation 12:12-17

As Satan and his hordes were driven from their place of ancient authority, the armies of Sabaoth completely drove them from the heavens, and their place was found no more.[90]

The voice of Gabriel thundered at the collapse of Satan's kingdom, "Now is come salvation, and strength, and the kingdom of our God, and the power of his Christ: for the accuser of our brethren is cast down, which accused them before our God day and night."

The heavens were silent, but for a moment, when the voice continued.

"Woe to the inhabiters of the earth and the seas for the devil is come down unto you, having great wrath, because he knows that the time he has left is short!"[91]

Although this battle was over and the armies of God rejoiced greatly, the arch commanders stood side by side with Prince Michael in quiet. They knew that although this war was done, there would have to be another, and this time, Christ would lead the charge, and his Church would do the fighting.

THE END

---

[90] Revelation 17:14
[91] Revelation 12:12

Acknowledgements

There are several people to whom I owe a debt of gratitude. To Bishop Hurley (Poppa) Bassett, Iowa Jurisdiction Bishop of the Church of God in Christ, what an honor to sit at the feet of a statesman in the gospel! Thank you for the section titles *Before It Was* and *When Shiloh Comes*.

To Mom Louise Penn, you've given me more than you can possibly imagine. I'm so grateful to have you in my life. Thank you for agreeing to read the manuscript of this book, for your insights and encouragement, and for assuring me that one day, this ministry-in-book form will be big!

To Elder Richard Yarbough, the magnitude of your encouragement and your belief in my gift as a writer is great. What a strange and divine consequence that God ordained you to read the original manuscript. May God bless you with a prophet's reward!

To my Pastor, Bishop Alexis A. Thomas of Phoenix, Arizona, when the words of this novel would not flow, your series on *Anointed to Finish!* carried me through discouragement and weariness. Thank you for wanting only the best for the sheep entrusted to your care.

Finally, to Pastor Gary L. Bush, Sr., years ago, you spoke Deuteronomy 29:29 into my spirit. The power of this one particular scripture gave me the boldness I needed to search out the mystery surrounding the fall of the most beautiful angel ever created.

To my Lord and Savior Jesus, without You, I am nothing.

www.ingramcontent.com/pod-product-compliance
Lightning Source LLC
LaVergne TN
LVHW091256080426
835510LV00007B/288